Best Practices of Elite Advisors

Best Practices of Elite Advisors

By Matt Oechsli and Stephen Boswell

Wealth Management Press
9800 Metcalf Ave.
Overland Park, KS 66212

First edition.

Designed and typeset by Sans Serif Inc., Saline,MI
Cover design by Rahul Chakraborty
Printed in the United States of America
ISBN: 978-0-9895509-0-1

Contents

Introduction

Today's New Normal

In the Virginia suburbs of D.C., Beth and Mary were enjoying a beautiful Sunday afternoon. They'd known each other for many years, and when their schedules and the weather permitted, they'd spend an afternoon visiting a local flea market. On this occasion, Mary asked Beth the following question, "*What does Bob actually do at XYZ Insurance Company?*"

Beth had been Bob's primary assistant for fifteen years, but this was the first time Mary had asked such a question. Beth's response was both conversational and simple, "*Basically, he oversees the financial affairs for a group of families in the D.C. area.*"

After a thoughtful pause, Mary responded, "*I thought he was an insurance agent.*"

"*We're still involved with insurance at times, but now our clients want us to oversee every aspect of their financial affairs,*" Beth replied.

"*It sounds like Bob would be perfect for my friend Jack,*" said Mary. "*Jack's very unhappy with his advisor at XYZ Firm. Do you think you could get Bob to meet with him?*"

A couple of meetings later, Jack became Bob's new $1.2 million client.

An Elite Advisor with an insurance background, Bob was extremely successful at selling life insurance, ranking in the top 25 of his company's 8,000-plus advisors. But Bob knew he was leaving a lot on the table with his affluent clients, so he got involved in the investment side of the business. He was perfectly equipped to become the "primary" financial advisor for his affluent clients.

As of this writing, Bob is three years into his transition from "great insurance agent" to "an advisor who oversees all of his clients' financial affairs."

It's a new world. Today's affluent investors don't care where a financial advisor launched his or her career—insurance, brokerage, accounting, banking, etc. Their only concern is what type of advisor you are today. The Great Recession created the perfect environment for advisors to re-brand. So, whether you're an insurance agent getting into wealth management, a stockbroker who's now involved with financial planning, or an accountant shifting from tax returns to ongoing tax advice, today's affluent recognize the need for your advice and guidance.

Bob, the insurance agent turned Elite Advisor, is a poster child for this kind of rebranding effort. One affluent client at a time, Bob has used the uncertainty and confusion produced by the financial crisis to expand his menu of services beyond life insurance. He started with financial planning, which led to gathering assets, which then led him to team with outside experts (estate planning attorneys) when necessary. The journey to Elite Advisor status is what this book is all about.

Our intention is to provide you with a roadmap, so that one client at a time, one sphere-of-influence at a time, one referral alliance partner at a time, elite status can be yours.

Nobody wants a stockbroker, insurance agent or any other one-dimensional financial professional advising them on their family's financial affairs, especially not the affluent. Today's affluent want a "family physician" of finances—someone who knows everything about their family, has a thorough understanding of finances, and who vets (and coordinates) other financial experts when necessary. They expect Ritz Carlton service with FedEx efficiency. Most important, they want to know this professional on a personal level.

Everything matters—the advisor's trustworthiness, depth and breadth of industry knowledge, quality of services, and relationship with clients.

If all of this seems daunting, you're right. It is. However, it *is* doable for any financial advisor willing to roll-up their sleeves. Our research has uncovered 14 criteria[1] that the affluent consider important in their professional relationships with financial advisors. Excel in addressing *all of them*, and you've entered the world of the new normal.

Today's Elite Advisors have done just that. They have worked feverishly to reposition their services, broaden the advisor/client relationship, connect with both spouses, and meet affluent clients' expectations for each of the 14 criteria. Because of their importance, we've taken to calling these criteria the ***14 Affluent Commandments.***

Use the *14 Affluent Commandments* Assessment below to determine where you stand relative to today's affluent expectations. This assessment should help you identify areas where you might need fine-tuning.

---

14 Affluent Commandments Assessment

1-Poor, 5-Excellent

Listening and understanding their family's needs	1 2 3 4 5
Being trustworthy and having their best interests at heart	1 2 3 4 5
Possessing a breadth and depth of industry knowledge	1 2 3 4 5
Being a problem solver	1 2 3 4 5
Providing personal, not mechanical communication	1 2 3 4 5
Overseeing their family's financial affairs, not marketing	1 2 3 4 5
Meeting investment performance expectations	1 2 3 4 5
Protecting them from downside risk	1 2 3 4 5
Making them fully aware of fees	1 2 3 4 5
Creating a financial plan and keeping it current	1 2 3 4 5
Using current technology	1 2 3 4 5
Coordinating and organizing their financial documents	1 2 3 4 5
Providing insurance solutions	1 2 3 4 5
Providing high-level personal service	1 2 3 4 5
Total Score:	__________

You don't need to tie yourself in knots over how you scored on the assessment. Nobody scores a perfect 70. Even today's Elite Advisors discover that they must raise their game to continue meeting affluent expectations. The difference between Elite Advisors and the masses is that the former recognize their weaknesses, address them, and continually strive to improve. It's a perfect example of their professionalism and concern for client relationships.

At a recent Affluent Focus Group[2] of clients with $500,000 to $10 million in investable assets, a discussion about client service elicited the following comments:

> *"My advisor only contacts me when I'm about to have a review."*
>
> *"I wish my advisor would communicate with me more frequently."*
>
> *"I resent getting passed off to someone junior."*
>
> *"I would like to have better access to my advisor."*
>
> *"If my advisor would do more than simply meet with me once a year to review my portfolio, if he was to do something with me that was fun, something social, I'd be happy to introduce him to my friends."*

What was interesting about the discussion was how it evolved. Initially, everyone claimed to be "satisfied" with their primary advisor ... that is, until we posed the following question:

> *"If you encountered a financial advisor you trusted and respected, and he or she offered to provide you with a second opinion on your family's finances, would you be interested?"*

The response was unanimous: all of the participants said they would be interested in having a second opinion in those circumstances. You heard comments like, "it just makes good business sense" and "why not." This from a group that was initially 100 percent satisfied.

This is client acquisition territory for Elite Advisors! It's obvious that these clients, though satisfied, are not really loyal. Why not? Anyone who would agree to a second opinion isn't truly loyal to their current advisor. Based on our data, we can also say their current advisor probably isn't meeting expectations for a number of the *14 Affluent Commandments.*

Our research is also quite clear about something every financial advisor should know: although most affluent investors would entertain a second opinion, they are NOT interested in making a lateral move.

What does that mean? Quite simply: if an advisor fails to present him or herself as a clearly superior alternative, the affluent prospect isn't interested. It's no different than purchasing a car. Very few people trade in an eight-year-old car with 110,000 miles for another eight-year-old car with 110,000 miles. If we are willing to go through the pain of making a change, it has to be for the better.

Once again, this underscores the importance of becoming an Elite Advisor. You have to meet the expectations of today's affluent to be successful in marketing your services to them. Word-of-mouth influence is *everything* in the new world of the affluent.

Working with the Elite

Over the past 30-plus years, The Oechsli Institute has had the privilege of working with some of the best financial advisors in the industry. Much of the coaching conducted by our group of 25 coaches is done with Elite Advisors. As you might expect, they're the most likely to seek professional coaching services and invest in their businesses. Many of these advisors are already very good at what they do. They manage their businesses well, service their clients at the highest levels, and bring in tremendous amounts of new assets. But they're always looking to get better.

Our coaching services create a win-win situation. It's a "win" for Elite Advisors because our coaching helps them grow in this new world. It's a "win" for The Oechsli Institute because this elite corps of advisors continues to teach us as much (if not more) than we teach them.

Our coaching of these elite practices gives us great insights into the types of research projects we should conduct. It helps frame the questions we ask, the trends we uncover, and the actionable information that results.

Our Research

Although we have a treasure chest of anecdotal evidence about the inner workings of these top advisors, we wanted to obtain empirical evidence as to what separates Elite Advisors from everyone else. Our objective was to make the findings usable, and by combining real-time data with hands-on coaching experience, we think we've hit the mark.

Our focus is on two areas: financial advisors and affluent families. We conduct parallel (simultaneous) research projects in both areas, which provide us with real-time data about affluent expectations of a financial professional, as well as corresponding data on what Elite Advisors are doing to meet these expectations. This research is the foundation of our articles, books, coaching and workshops.

Affluent Families

Over the years we've surveyed thousands of affluent families from the U.S. Census Bureau's top quintile of income earners. We make certain these families hail from every region of the country; have a minimum of $250,000 in investable assets, and work with at least one financial professional.

This research provides us with the answers to questions such as:

- What qualities do affluent investors seek from financial advisors?
- Who do affluent investors trust? Who don't they trust?
- What factors into an affluent investor's loyalty to their advisor?
- What level of service and services are Elite Advisors offering?
- What type of communication do affluent investors want? How often?

Our research identified two major trends, which we labeled *Macro Affluent Shifts.*[3] These transformative shifts required advisors to make substantial adjustments to their practices in order to acquire and maintain ideal client relationships.

The first *macro shift* is based on gender. Today's affluent women are becoming much more involved in the relationship with their family's financial advisor. The days of male financial advisors dealing exclusively with the male of the affluent household are winding down. Today's affluent female wants to be part of the conversation.

The second *macro shift* concerns the nature of the advisor/client relationship. Today's affluent investor no longer wants a business-only relationship with the advisor. They want their advisor to know them on a personal level—and vice versa.

These two shifts are having a profound impact on whether or not investor expectations are being met and both highlight how fragile trust has become. Elite Advisors have embraced change. They've not only addressed the *macro shifts;* they're capitalizing on them, which is why success continues to come their way.

Four-Lane Advisor Highway

Imagine a highway whose only motorists are financial advisors. This highway has four lanes, and as with most highways, some lanes are moving faster than others. This four-lane highway represents the industry today. Some advisors are excelling, while many others aren't moving forward as quickly as they'd like. While it's possible to change lanes, it requires a focused and concerted effort.

Which lane are you in? Which lane would you like to be in? Let's take a drive . . .

> ***Lane One:*** We call this the breakdown lane. In this lane, you see advisors who refuse to change and as a result have been paralyzed by the financial crisis. They're not sure what to do, so they're not doing much of anything. This is a sad state of affairs, since many of these advisors are veterans who once enjoyed higher levels of success.
>
> Some of these advisors have lost personal wealth; some have lost clients. Worse, many have grown cynical, negative and passionless (beware of road rage!). They are resisting change, blind to the Macro Affluent Shifts, and aren't doing much to adapt to the new environment.

Lane Two: This lane is full of financial advisors who would like to improve their businesses, but have yet to recognize our new world, so their energies are being directed to the wrong activities.

They have yet to change how they interact with clients, and they've added little (if any) value to their deliverables. They often attempt to market themselves using the tactics of yesteryear (cold calling, direct mail, seminars)—tactics that no longer work.

These advisors are more active, but they're just doing more of the same. It's almost as though they are waiting expectantly, or maybe simply hoping, that everything will return to "normal." They don't realize that the financial crisis has created a new normal.

Lane Two advisors are living, breathing examples of the insanity quote attributed to Einstein: *insanity* is continuing to do the same thing and expecting a different result. Because their activities so rarely bear fruit, these financial advisors often find themselves skidding into the breakdown lane—Lane One.

Lane Three: Fewer advisors are driving in this lane compared with Lanes One and Two. The advisors traveling in Lane Three recognize that the crisis has created a new world and that they need to change. They have recognized the Macro Affluent Shifts, and understand that success hinges on managing the relationships with current clients (relationship management). They realize that these relationships involve both spouses; that they must add new services, and that they must penetrate clients' affluent centers-of-influence (relationship marketing).

The main challenge confronting these advisors is they lack the skills necessary for working with today's skeptical affluent investor. When they attempt to add new services or strengthen current client relationships, they make several common mistakes. They talk too much, they talk too much about business, they talk too much about investments, and they usually do most of this talking to the *husband* of the household. Unwittingly, they sound like the same pre-Great Recession advisor who routinely ignored the spouse. This is not what the affluent want.

These advisors make similar mistakes in relationship marketing. They're too quick to discuss business, which comes across as salesy. They talk too much about investments, which makes them sound like stockbrokers. They talk too much about themselves, which is boring. Basically, they talk too much. When these advisors offer a second opinion, they find themselves on the receiving end of a polite "no thanks." If they pursue this trajectory for any length of time, these advisors end up in Lane One.

Although these financial advisors are well-intentioned, their skill deficits keep them from achieving the results that Elite Advisors are enjoying.

Lane Four: This is where you'll find Elite Advisors. This is *their* lane. They have re-positioned and (when necessary) re-branded their services with existing clients. They communicate well with both spouses, routinely socialize with them, and always keep current with their clients' needs. For these reasons, Elite Advisors are perceived as the primary advisors to their affluent families—trusted advisors not unlike the "consiglieres" of *The Godfather* movies (without the mafia associations, of course).

Elite Advisors excel in relationship marketing. They've worked hard to master the art of affluent sales, enabling them to penetrate their clients' spheres-of-influence without coming across like high-pressure salespeople. They easily develop friendships that, in many instances, become client relationships. They are true rainmakers. This select corps of advisors is acquiring a larger pool of assets at a faster pace than anyone has done before.

This book is all about Lane Four. Our goal is simple: we have chronicled the best practices of Elite Advisors in the following chapters as a guide for any financial advisor interested in achieving greater success with affluent investors. We want to see more financial advisors in Lane Four.

Defining Elite Advisors

Before going any further, let's review our definition of "Elite." In our most recent research, we have identified Elite Advisors as those who:

- Brought in five or more $1mm+ clients (per advisor) over the past year.
- Lost three or fewer clients over the past year.
- Reported being "Very Satisfied" with their career.
- Excelled in the 14 Affluent Commandments.

In total, 6.9% of financial advisors are considered Elite; meeting the minimum requirements for entry into the Elite Advisor club.[4] Many of the stories we'll share with you are from Elite Advisors and Elite Teams who far surpass these figures. They are recognized by their firms, their peers, and the industry as being the best of the best. We know you'll find their best practices useful.

The prototypical big producer of yesteryear may not be elite today. Sadly, it's hard to teach some "old-dogs" Elite Advisor tricks, and this resistance to change has landed many in Lane One. Hence, we felt the need for a book of this nature. It's our belief that the best way for a financial advisor to enjoy a successful career in today's world is by modeling the best practices of today's Elite Advisors.

As you read through these chapters, you'll undoubtedly experience some "Ah-Ha!" moments, but much of what we'll communicate will be intuitive or common sense. We've learned from years of coaching financial advisors that every reader will enjoy the book at a different pace—and at a different place in their professional life. No two advisors are alike.

We are convinced that, with a little fine-tuning and a strong work ethic, opportunity awaits every advisor who's serious about plying his or her craft with affluent investors.

1

The Relationship Management / Relationship Marketing Nexus™

Factoid: Clients with a business and social relationship with their advisor gave twice as many referrals over the past year as those with a purely business relationship.[1]

Imagine socializing with your top clients, strengthening the relationships and being introduced to their friends. Imagine doing all this in a friendly, non-threatening environment. Well, *this* is the world of today's Elite Advisors.

For today's Elite Advisor, relationship management and relationship marketing are inextricably linked. This connection is what prompted us to coin the term: *The Relationship Management / Relationship Marketing Nexus™*.

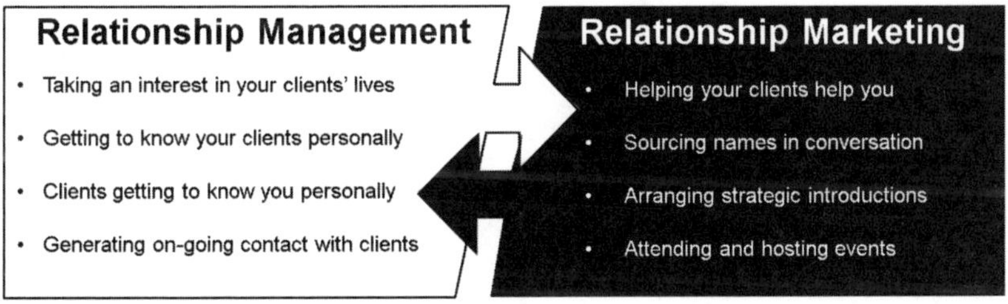

As arduous as this might appear, it's actually rather simple, at least in concept. Elite Advisors have discovered that by adhering to the two

Macro Affluent Shifts and getting social with their affluent clients (husband and wife), they strengthen these relationships while at the same time meeting friends and colleagues of their clients. When this occurs in social settings, which is often the case, relationship management and relationship marketing are functioning in tandem. It doesn't get any better than that.

Building and nurturing relationships is innate to all but the most dysfunctional people. But doing this with strategic intent requires a unique set of skills, including interpersonal skills, sales skills and discipline. All of these can be learned and refined.

The following example was shared by a participant in one of our live events:

> "I went with one of my top clients, husband and wife, to a social function at our club. My intention was for the husband to introduce me to his associate. He gave me a little background on his associate, so when he introduced me I was able to develop rapport by getting him talking about his son's tennis. He introduced me to his wife in the midst of talking about their son's tennis—a conversation she was eager to join as a proud mother. Not a word was mentioned about business until his wife finally asked how I knew Bob (the client). My response was simply, 'I help Bob and Mary oversee their family's financial affairs.' That grabbed her attention, so I added, 'Just guiding them through this mess.' She looked at her husband, and suggested that we meet."

This scenario, as simple as it might appear, contains seven "Elite Advisor" relationship marketing insights:

Insight #1: Getting Social

We have an Elite Advisor socializing with a top client *couple.* This is what relationship management is all about. Today, it's rare to find an affluent client who will socialize with a financial advisor if this client doesn't like, trust and respect the advisor on a professional level. This form of socializing is a critical factor for strengthening client loyalty with both husband and wife. It's also the most natural door-opener for penetrating affluent spheres-of-influence.

Insight # 2: Sourcing Names

Not only did this Elite Advisor organize a social get-together with husband and wife, he had already identified one of the husband's colleagues as a prospect. Elite Advisors don't ask for referrals, because they're aware that this leads to awkward conversations. Seven out of 10 affluent clients have a negative reaction when asked for a referral.[3] Instead, they "source" the names of people connected to their affluent clients, and strive for a personal introduction.

Insight #3: Intelligence Gathering

Our Elite Advisor knew how he was going to develop rapport with his affluent client's colleague upon being introduced. Like all good relationship marketers, he did his homework by getting a little background on this colleague from the client. That's how he knew about the son playing competitive tennis.

Insight #4: Strategic Intent

Nothing was left to chance. Our Elite Advisor approached the social event with a game plan, which we refer to as "strategic intent." He was going to socialize with his client, knowing that his client was comfortable with the idea of introducing him to a colleague. It was his skill as an Elite Advisor that allowed him to naturally orchestrate the process.

Insight #5: Develop Rapport

Thanks to his intelligence gathering, the advisor was able to develop rapport naturally and quickly. Getting the prospect talking about his son's tennis was a perfect way to get him talking about something he loved to discuss—his son. Getting introduced to the prospect's wife as she joined the conversation about their son's tennis was also very natural. There was no mention of business. This may seem counterintuitive, but the less business discussed in these situations, the more business is obtained.

Insight #6: Seamless Value Proposition

When the conversation caused the prospect's wife to become curious about the advisor's relationship with her husband's colleague, the Elite Advisor was prepared. His response painted a short and simple word picture that avoided industry jargon and planted a seed of dissatisfaction.

Insight #7: Mini-Closing

The Elite Advisor's sales skills were so refined that he was able to read dissatisfaction in the wife's body language, which was disguised as interest. From there, he remained silent (less talking; more impact), which prompted the prospect's wife to suggest they get together. Everything about the encounter was non-threatening. In this instance, Bob didn't have to suggest a meeting to review their family's finances; we refer to this as a "mini-close." The prospect closed for him.

These 7 Insights are illustrative of the "perfect storm" the financial crisis has created for Elite Advisors to prospect within social circles. The conversation from beginning to end (insights 5–7) took no longer than ten minutes, and it involved both spouses. Cell phone numbers were exchanged, a time, date and place for meeting were established, and everyone switched gears back to the festivities at hand.

The scenario may appear ideal, but it's something Elite Advisors live almost every day. It may appear simple, but it's far from easy to pull off. It requires a high level of skill and work.

Understanding today's affluent, in all their idiosyncrasies, is a work in progress but it's imperative for any advisor who wants success in this marketplace. For instance, the number one pet peeve voiced in our affluent focus groups was lack of communication. The following phrase, pulled straight from our *14 Affluent Commandments*, makes the point well:

I want my financial advisor to oversee my family's financial affairs, not market his practice.

When this is combined with the fact that 83 percent[1] of our affluent respondents would introduce their financial advisor (with whom they have both a business and social relationship) to someone in their spheres-of-influence, it becomes apparent that a strong personal relationship is a major component of their willingness to help their advisor acquire new clients. This is despite the fact that they want their advisor focused on them, not on marketing their services.

We find this all quite fascinating. On the one hand, today's affluent want all the love and attention (relationship management), while on the other hand, if they're getting what they want from their advisor, they are very willing to open the doors to their spheres-of-influence (relationship marketing).

Today's financial advisor must be perceived as the consummate professional; working hard to address affluent clients' needs in this new world. However, the consummate professional who excels in relationship management is not necessarily a rainmaker. Rainmaking is about mastering the art of affluent sales. It requires attention to detail, detective work and seamless sales skills that are applied to client and prospect alike. Elite Advisors don't embarrass affluent clients by discussing business prematurely or by talking too much, especially in social settings. They are masters of developing rapport with prospects. They know how to make people feel comfortable.

When relationship marketing is broken into its component parts, it is a very delicate process. In many ways, it's analogous to a golf swing. The pros make it look simple, but it requires a lot of practice and attention to detail. With one minor flaw, the ball lands in the rough.

Advisors' flaws take many forms—talking too much, thinking they're developing rapport when they're actually being a bore (or a boor), failing to connect with the female of the household, not doing their homework and not recognizing opportunities (to name a few). Many advisors still don't understand the value of socializing with affluent clients, while others don't realize the importance of involving both spouses. The majority of today's advisors need basic training in affluent sales skills.

Getting Social with Clients

By now, we're sure you've gotten the message: any advisor serious about targeting the affluent had better learn how to get social with client and spouse. As we've become increasingly addicted to our digital toys (iPads, iPhones, et al.) and with social media now taking center stage, it's easy to lean too heavily on impersonal communication. However, our research tells us that getting to know someone personally happens best when you're face-to-face in a non-business venue.

You wouldn't think socializing would be a big problem for advisors. But it never ceases to amaze us how uncomfortable many become when they even *contemplate* prospecting in affluent social circles. Fresh in our mind is a workshop we conducted for the top advisors of a major financial firm. The focus was on building a 21st century financial practice based on the best practices of Elite Advisors. When we got to the part of the program where we discussed that today's affluent want both a business and social relationship and that involving both spouses is important, nervous questions began pouring out . . .

> *"How do you socialize with your clients?"*
> *"Is it appropriate to discuss business at all?"*
> *"If I haven't involved my client's spouse before, how do I get started?"*

We could go on, but you get the picture. Our response was to re-emphasize the following factoids:

- Clients with a purely business relationship gave an average of 0.97 referrals last year.
- Clients with a business and social relationship gave an average of 1.95 referrals last year.[1]

There it is—in black and white. Advisors receive twice as many referrals by socializing with affluent clients. This supports what we've learned from our rainmaking research: social prospecting is a key component of an Elite Advisor's marketing plan.

After digesting this information, the questions continued and it was obvious that we'd just lowered the comfort level in the room.

> *"When do you talk about business?"*
> *"What social activities should you engage in?"*
> *"Is it more difficult for women to prospect socially?"*

As we explained to these advisors, Elite Advisors view this as a gift: they can schmooze with their top clients, meet clients' friends in a non-threatening environment, develop rapport and build personal relationships with the friends, and then turn those friends into clients.

In the chapters that follow, we will get into more detail regarding the inner workings of relationship management and relationship marketing. You will begin to notice how it is the fabric that is woven throughout the book. Why? Because it's at the core of today's Elite Advisor—it's how they roll.

Key Takeaways:

- Create a schedule for your personal contact with each of your affluent clients, husband and wife.
- Let your clients get to know you on a personal level. You have to give to get.
- Create a plan for getting social with your clients. It should be as well-planned as your client review process.
- When arranging introductions, keep it social. It's easier for clients to introduce you to a friend or colleague at a social event.
- Always do your homework when attending a social event; who is attending, who do I want to meet, and what do I need to know about them in order to develop rapport.

2

The Elite Advisor Model

Factoid: Only 6.9% of today's financial advisors are traveling in Lane 4.[4]

Elite Advisors are cut from a different cloth. Not only do they meet the expectations of their affluent clients, they consistently acquire new affluent clients, run their practices efficiently, spend time with their families, and provide leadership in the community. They're not perfect—every Elite Advisor has weaknesses—but their actions are worth emulating. Our goal is to use their best practices as a model that any advisor can use to dramatically enhance performance.

The Great Recession has been a game changer for everyone, but especially financial advisors. As the world continues to digest Wall Street's shenanigans and the government's complicity, profound changes are occurring in the relationship between financial advisors and their affluent clients. These changes are woven through the seven components of our model.

ELITE ADVISOR

- Leadership
- Affluent Loyalty
- Wealth Management
- Business Development
- Practice Management
- Lifelong Learner
- Balance

Leadership

During the financial crisis, when it seemed the whole financial industry was falling into the abyss, Jack met personally with each of his affluent clients. His objective was twofold: (1) determine their level of anxiety and (2) demonstrate emotional confidence in the midst of the storm. "My clients were so grateful," Jack explained. "Even though I didn't have any immediate solution, I assured them that I was monitoring their situations carefully and would keep them posted if we needed to make any changes. I basically instructed them not to panic."

That was leadership.

Jack had a similar conversation with his support staff, because he didn't want them to worry about their jobs and transfer personal anxiety to the clients. This strategy paid off handsomely. "One of my physician clients called in a panic. He and three colleagues, all clients, wanted to close their accounts and move into cash. My assistant was able to talk him off the cliff and schedule a lunch meeting for all four clients. During the lunch, I was able to calm the waters. Nobody went to cash, and to this day, I continue to receive thanks."

Jack is an Elite Advisor who displayed courage and leadership under fire.

Financial advisor leadership (and a lack thereof) was never more apparent than in the midst of the crisis. Financial institutions were going out of business, and the media was fanning the flames of fear by constantly forecasting an apocalypse. Meanwhile, Elite Advisors were leading their support staff ("It's going to be OK"), meeting with clients and making appropriate adjustments, repositioning their services, and helping guide everyone through the crisis—emotionally and financially.

This was extremely painful and time consuming, but it also prompted them to provide the same level of support and guidance to the friends, colleagues and extended family members of their affluent clients. Leadership at this level involves high-level sales skills—precisely the skills that rainmakers need to segue into "acquisition mode."

Business Development

Once upon a time, Sheila never socialized with clients. She was uncomfortable outside of business settings, and vowed never to mix business with pleasure. But *that* was pre-Great Recession Sheila. With guidance from a coach, she not only learned how to socialize with her affluent clients, she began hosting intimate client events. Once a month, she would hold a "fun" event attended by a few client couples, each bringing a friend. At these non-business venues, she refined her sales skills to the point where she could offer second opinions without seeming "pushy."

Today, she is acquiring new assets at a higher dollar level and a faster rate than ever before in her 23-year career. She has averaged between $30 and $40 million of new assets a year over the last three years. *Sheila is an Elite Advisor.*

Elite Advisors are acquiring new affluent clients while simultaneously repositioning their services with existing clients. Sheila repositioned her services to one affluent client at a time while working to *acquire* one new affluent client at a time. Essentially, this repositioning involved expanding the services she offered, which enabled her to consolidate assets that some of these clients were holding elsewhere. Although the precipitous decline in the markets negatively impacted production, Elite Advisors recognize that new client acquisition and consolidating the assets of current clients are the lifeblood of business growth.

Elite Advisors have a business plan, specific new-asset and new-client acquisition goals, as well as a metrics scorecard that lets them measure their progress. As Sheila demonstrated with her "fun" intimate client events, Elite Advisors understand the connection between relationship marketing (business development) and relationship management (client loyalty).

Client Loyalty

"Mr. Big," as he's affectionately known by his advisor, is an affluent client and a power player. He knows everyone who's anyone, and needs to be handled with kid gloves. Robert, the advisor we are coaching, was introduced to him by a client, and the timing was fortuitous. Mr. Big wasn't happy with his current advisor. Six weeks later, after firing his advisor, Mr. Big was one of Robert's top clients.

"I knew this relationship was going to be a challenge, because he soured on his advisor over some trivial issue regarding service," said Robert. "However, it became obvious that *Mrs.* Big was the one who was really unhappy with the previous advisor. From that point on, my objective was to get to know *Mrs. Big* and transform her into an ally."

Robert was able to get onto Mr. Big's Christmas party invite list months before the event. It started by obtaining permission from Mr. Big to invite Mrs. Big to lunch. After Mrs. Big accepted the invitation, Robert hired a driver to pick him up at the office, and Mrs. Big at her house. In addition, Robert's assistant had him bring a bouquet of flowers.

The lunch couldn't have gone better. Mrs. Big wasn't always aware of Mr. Big's financial planning activities, and she felt left out. Robert also discovered that because most people were intimidated by Mrs. Big, they rarely socialized with her without Mr. Big in tow.

Mrs. Big loved the flowers and talked about the floral arrangements she was considering for the Christmas party. As they discussed the party, Mrs. Big spontaneously invited Robert and his wife. Thus began Robert's loyalty process with Mr. and Mrs. Big.

Between the initial lunch and the Christmas party, Robert and Mrs. Big chatted numerous times, not about investments, but about the party. Robert had a $200 floral arrangement delivered to the house, which Mrs. Big displayed prominently in the foyer. She showed the display to all the guests as they entered the house, expressing her appreciation for both the bouquet and Robert's thoughtfulness. From that point forward, Mrs. Big became Robert's advocate. She introduced him to everyone at the party as "the wonderful gentleman who brought me that beautiful bouquet in the foyer."

As of this writing, Robert has acquired four clients and $36.5 million of new assets, thanks to Mrs. Big's introductions. Not only have Mr. & Mrs. Big become loyal clients, Robert is now a fixture within their affluent spheres-of-influence.

As Robert's example illustrates, loyal affluent clients are an Elite Advisor's acre of diamonds. The affluent make major purchase decisions through word-of-mouth and they trust the recommendations of their friends, colleagues and family members. We have found that a loyal affluent family has seven spheres-of-influence: family members, friends, colleagues, organizations, professionals, people with whom they "play," and their neighbors. Although each of these spheres-of-influence (more on this later) isn't necessarily full of affluent prospects, nearly every client can introduce you if approached properly.

Wealth Management

Michael built his career as an astute investment advisor. He personally managed his clients' portfolios, taking considerable pride in his work. However, the Great Recession hit him hard and he recognized he needed to rebrand himself with affluent clients. He also realized that he had to expand his service offerings because affluent clients were interested in *planning*.

Since he wasn't a CFP and had never done any planning, Michael partnered with a young advisor (and CFP) in order to offer planning to top clients. While completing their first joint plan, the young advisor identified an insurance solution with key tax advantages. The net result: a six-figure commission, a happy client, a young advisor who's now a permanent part of Michael's team, and an expanded menu of wealth management services.

As we mentioned earlier, advisors must be able to meet the expectations of today's affluent on all fronts. No more fancy elevator speeches: today's advisor must have a depth *and* breadth of knowledge and bring in outside experts when necessary.

Our research is quite clear: the affluent are looking beyond someone to help them invest in the stock market. The financial world has become so convoluted, so connected and confusing, that today's affluent want a single go-to advisor overseeing every moving part in their lives—from investments to taxes to refinancing to protection to cash management. And the female of today's affluent household has higher expectations than her husband. If her expectations aren't met, regardless of what the husband thinks, the advisor/client relationship is extremely vulnerable.

Practice Management

Gerry discovered the realities of contemporary practice management the hard way. He lost a $4 million client. Why? He didn't nurture personal relationships. He was using mechanical contact, email and ghost-written e-letters, as his primary mode of communication. He thought solid practice management, and even smart business, consisted of an automated system for maintaining client contact.

Without realizing it, Gerry's mechanical process enticed a top client's wife to attend a dinner where one of his firm's analysts was speaking. When the event concluded, Mrs. Affluent Client approached Gerry, thrust her finger in his face and said, "You owe me. I didn't understand a word this guy said! That's what we pay *you* for."

Three weeks later, the woman's husband told Gerry that they were moving their account. It was during this conversation that Gerry discovered that the man's wife had become convinced that Gerry didn't really know them, and that he didn't really care.

Elite Advisors run their businesses like a business, but treat their affluent clients like people. Every aspect of their practice management is designed to provide a Ritz Carlton level of personalized service with a FedEx level of efficiency. Because problem-solving and clear communications are essential criteria for strengthening client loyalty, effective practice management is more vital than ever before. The wife of his $4 million ex-client felt they were just a number.

Effective practice management requires clarity in roles and responsibilities, effective delegation, open communication and accountability. Only by establishing good practice management processes can Elite Advisors devote enough time to affluent clients and their spheres-of-influence.

Lifelong Learner

The examples above illustrate lifelong learning in action. Those advisors, including Gerry (we hope), have made changes to how they manage affluent client relationships and how they market to new clients. In every instance, learning was a requirement. Whether it's getting involved with financial planning and insurance solutions, learning to socialize with clients, or recognizing the importance of involving the female of the affluent household, these changes required an open-minded advisor. Elite Advisors are open-minded lifelong learners.

Nobody wants to be treated by a physician who isn't current on the latest developments in their field of medicine. The same holds true for today's affluent investor and their financial advisor. Clients want someone who is open-minded and well-read. They don't expect you to be an expert in every aspect of finances, but they do expect you to connect them with the appropriate expert.

As a by-product, a broad knowledge base enables Elite Advisors to be more effective in social conversation, which is where much of their marketing takes place.

Balance

Standing in the foyer of an upscale seafood restaurant, Terry is wearing one of his new custom-tailored suits, complete with a pocket square in his breast pocket and a fedora in hand. Over the past year, Terry lost forty pounds by changing his habits. He hired a personal trainer, began exercising at 6:00 a.m. five days a week, and has become a healthy eater. No more desserts, fried foods, soft drinks or refined carbohydrates.

His energy and confidence have dramatically improved. The family eats better, and health and fitness habits are a frequent topic of conversation. Just as important, Terry has evolved into an Elite Advisor. He acquired $18 million in new assets the previous year, his one-year record, and hired a personal assistant just for himself—he no longer shares an assistant.

When discussing the transformation, Terry stresses that getting in shape created a balance that was missing in his life. Today, he spends more quality time with his family, is more focused at work, and is addicted to healthy eating and regular exercise.

The new-normal has taken all of us back to basics. Family values are more important, living within our means has become a priority, as has taking care of ourselves mentally and physically. This is not to suggest that all Elite Advisors are paragons of balance. But they *have* made substantial progress. Today's affluent investors want advisors who are congruent with the advice they provide—i.e., they don't want the "family physician" to be wildly out of shape.

As Terry tells anyone who'll listen, being an Elite Advisor requires a lot of energy, and balance creates more energy. It also helps that Elite Advisors are able to market their services in affluent circles by skillfully mixing business with pleasure. (You'll recall that Terry was in the foyer of that seafood restaurant waiting for a client. He was having a healthy non-business lunch.)

At first glance this Elite Advisor model can be very intimidating. As you're about to discover, it's quite the opposite. It's been our experience in coaching to this model that your actions have a ripple effect, and improvement builds upon improvement. It's the old adage; progress begets progress. So buckle-up and get ready to plunge into the *business development* component.

Key Takeaways

- The Elite Advisor model is a template to assist advisors in improving. No financial services practice is perfect, but the best advisors are always looking to refine their operations.
- The professional requirements of today's financial advisor are much greater, both in terms of financial solutions offered, depth and breadth of knowledge required, and service expectations.
- Each component in the Elite Advisor model has been shaped by this Great Recession. Advisors should take an honest self-assessment of their current status within each component.
- There are few role models traveling in Lane 4, less than 7% of the general population of financial advisors.

3

Business Development

Factoid: If you have a business and social relationship with them, 83% of your affluent clients would personally introduce you to a friend, family member or colleague.[1]

Imagine talking to an affluent client and shifting the conversation to something personal, such as "Who'd you play golf with last weekend?" Does this appear a bit out of character? It shouldn't. This is the type of every day conversation that enables Elite Advisors to uncover the names of real people within their affluent clients' spheres-of-influence. In this example you, as the advisor, would gain insight into your client's golfing buddies. Not too complicated, is it? Every financial advisor should be capable of having that conversation. We refer to this high-impact activity as *sourcing names.*

The reality is that every financial advisor can replicate the rain-making success of Elite Advisors. Our research tells us that this simple conversation is one of the key components of acquiring affluent clients.

Elite Advisors are masters at sourcing names as they have learned to ask the "who" question in a conversational manner. *Who* did you play golf with last weekend? *Who* else is on that committee? *Who* are you watching the Super Bowl with? Once names are sourced through such natural conversation, these advisors do a little homework in the form of gathering information about this person. From there they set about to get personally introduced.

7 Spheres-of-influence

Our research tells us that each affluent client has *7 Spheres-of-influence.* These 7 Spheres include family, friends, colleagues, neighbors, recreational contacts, organizational contacts, and professionals. These represent an Elite Advisor's acre of diamonds. We created this model to help advisors think more broadly about the connection potential of each client or COI. It's been quite helpful in coaching advisors to source more names.

We recognize that every sphere-of-influence will not be full of affluent prospect opportunities, but it's been our experience that there will be more than enough who qualify to make this exercise very worthwhile. We have also found this model helpful to support personnel in their efforts to uncover names within an affluent client's spheres-of-influence.

Using the model above, ask yourself the following questions . . .

1. If you were to map the spheres-of-influence of your top 25 clients, how many names would you be able to connect? For

most advisors, this exercise is a real challenge at first. They haven't developed the habit of sourcing names. We have found that one conversation at a time, with the right focus, you'll be able to put real names into these spheres rather quickly.

2. If you were to chart your own spheres-of-influence, how many total connections could you list? How many have the means to conduct business with you?

Here's the deal. If you can source three to four names a week from your affluent clients, then follow-up in the proper time frame and ask for a personal introduction, you're on your way to becoming an Elite Advisor.

Business Development Research

Only a fraction of advisors are bringing in five or more clients with $1 million-plus in investable assets per year (or comparable benchmarks for those focused on insurance and other solutions). We've studied this group extensively and have been able to determine which marketing activities they use most frequently, which activities bring in the most new business, and which activities they avoid. The following chart speaks volumes:

Average New $1mm+ Clients per Prospecting Method[4]

	Non-elite	Elite
Referral alliances	0.8	2.9
Introductions	0.8	2.5
Indirect referrals	0.5	1.5
Strategic networking	0.6	1.4
Client events	0.2	0.9
Direct referrals	0.3	0.8
Seminar	0.2	0.6
Cold calling	0.1	0.1
Online lead	0.1	0.1
Direct mail	0	0

Oechsli Institute Financial Advisor Research

A quick glance at this data highlights the effective marketing activities in today's environment: referral alliances, introductions, indirect referrals, networking and intimate events. Indirect referrals are those generated purely from good service, not directly asking for referrals.

These are not overly complicated strategies, but many advisors fall short in their execution. An Elite Advisor and a non-Elite Advisor can both be asking for personal introductions, with only one of them seeing results. The skill component makes all the difference. This is why we've dedicated the balance of this chapter to understanding *why* and *how* these tactics work. What appears simple at first glance becomes a work of art with further study.

Marketing Activities

Personal Introductions

The power of word-of-mouth influence within affluent spheres-of-influence should never be underestimated. The fact is that it has continued to gain importance in how the affluent make major decisions. They talk to people whom they trust and respect. This transference of opinions is having a tremendous impact on advisors attempting to market their services to the affluent.

Our affluent research tells us how today's affluent initially discovered their current financial advisor[1]...

1. Introduction from another professional
2. Introduction from a family member
3. I approached him/her directly
4. Introduction from a friend

Personal introduction was number one by far. For all practical purposes, this is how the affluent first came into contact with their advisor, not how they made their final decision to become a client. The final decision had two key ingredients; 1) Recommendation from someone they trust, 2) Reputation of the advisor.

What is important for advisors to understand is that "word-of-mouth influence" is woven throughout the initial discovery and final selection process. It's also important to realize that when an affluent client personally introduces their financial advisor to someone, even in a social setting, the unsaid message is "This is a trustworthy person." It serves as a tacit recommendation.

That said, upon getting personally introduced, it's incumbent upon the advisor to make a good first impression. This requires seamless sales skills and usually occurs by developing rapport with the new acquaintance (prospect). Elite Advisors accomplish this by getting this new prospect to talk about themselves, with little or no discussion of business. Why shouldn't you discuss business at this critical juncture? Because, by the mere nature of being personally introduced by an affluent client, you're also being silently vetted—you're credible. There is no need for an advisor to feel compelled to talk about their services at this stage.

Elite Advisors understand all of this, which is why for them, it's really quite simple. They source names, wait a couple of weeks so they don't appear too aggressive, then call their client and ask to be personally introduced.

Asking to be introduced to someone that's connected to one of your affluent clients is the polar opposite of asking an affluent client for a referral. Yet because advisors have been taught for so many years to ask for referrals, they tend to think of referrals and introductions as being one-in-the same. They are not!

Chris, a financial advisor we know, recently started asking for referrals again. It had been years since he tried it, and he wanted to give this tactic another shot. The response by the first client he asked stopped this new referral program in its tracks. The client simply said, "Wow, times must be tough!"

In our workshops, whenever we ask advisors how their affluent clients *feel* when asked for a referral, the responses are always similar: awkward, used, uncomfortable, put upon, etc. When asked how they feel when they ask for a referral, advisors' answers are virtually the same: they don't like asking for referrals. Unfortunately, "asking for referrals" is still promoted as an effective sales tactic. Here is the truth—straight from our affluent research:

- 7 out of 10 feel uncomfortable when asked for a referral[3]

They're uncomfortable because this "simple" referral request puts the onus on the client and prompts a multitude of other questions:

- Who do I know that has money?
- Who do I know who isn't happy with his or her current advisor?
- Who won't be put off by me giving out their name to this pushy advisor?

And then your affluent client replies with something along the lines of. . . .

"Let me get back to you." (In other words, "No, thanks.")

This tactic has been around a long time, but has no place in the world of the affluent. There are far more sophisticated ways of achieving the desired result (meeting new prospects through current clients). Elite Advisors orchestrate these connections in a way that *builds* the relationship between them and the client.

With personal introductions, the data works in your favor:

- 83 percent will introduce you to a specific person if asked (if you have a business and social relationship)
- 66 percent will introduce you to a specific person if asked (if you have a purely business relationship[1])

There's a big difference in the willingness to introduce, a seventeen percentage-point gap, between advisors with purely business relationships with affluent clients and advisors who've taken the time to also develop a social relationship. This is the essence of the *Relationship Management / Relationship Marketing Nexus™*. The more personal an advisor becomes with an affluent client, the more natural it becomes to source names, and the more willing the affluent client is to make a personal introduction when asked.

An important point to remember is that by asking for an introduction, you are helping your client help you by identifying a specific person you'd like to meet. This is the heart of the introduction process.

You're not asking "who do you know?" You're doing the detective work yourself (sourcing names in conversation or online) and thinking about how this introduction might take place, before even thinking about calling your client.

The standard timeline protocol is to wait a couple of weeks from the date the name was sourced (you never want to appear too eager), and then call your client to request an introduction. The wording should be direct and concise: "Bob, you mentioned that you have drinks after work with a colleague on Fridays. I'd like to meet him. Could I tag along next week?" Of course, if you don't drink, you can ask to be introduced by other means. Lunches, dinners, sporting events, and other similar functions work just as well.

In fact, we've uncovered 10 variations of this introduction approach—there are probably 10 more. Use these to stimulate your introduction creativity:

1. **Direct**—"Matt, I'd like to meet your colleague Stephen. What would be the best way for us all to get together socially?"
2. **Two-Step Indirect**—"Matt, you mentioned you spend a lot of time with Stephen at work. Does he know that you and I work together?" (Pause) "Great, I would love the opportunity to meet him."
3. **Recreational**—"Matt, we're looking to get a foursome together for golf this Saturday. Would you want to join us? (Pause) Do you think your colleague Stephen would want to play?"
4. **Social**—"Matt, why don't you invite Stephen and his wife to join us at the club's wine tasting this Friday night?"
5. **Compelling Reason**—"Matt, you mentioned Stephen's going to retire soon. You probably should introduce me to him—just to make certain he's got his bases covered. That's exactly what I do."
6. **Situational**—"Matt, are Stephen and Heidi going to be at the fundraiser this Saturday night?"

7. **Tag Along**—"Matt, next time you and Stephen go fishing, would you mind if I tagged along? I would really like to meet him."
8. **Strategic Placement**—"Matt, I'd love to attend the fundraiser, but could you make certain I'm sitting next to Stephen and Heidi?"
9. **Spontaneous Situational**—"Matt, is that your colleague Stephen with his wife over there? Could you introduce me?"
10. **Online Profiling**—"Matt, I saw that you're connected to Stephen Boswell online—how well do you know him? Could you introduce me?" (follow up statement) "Let me know if you ever want to meet any of my connections."

In reality, if you become proficient with two or three of these techniques, you'll have enough tools to be in lane four with Elite Advisors.

The secret is arranging the personal introduction in a social venue. Why? For starters, it's more comfortable for your client to simply make the connection, not sell your services. Plus, it's easier for you to develop rapport with a prospect when business isn't on the agenda. This type of social meet-n-greet will require a bit of brainstorming with an affluent client about how, when and where this personal introduction will occur. However, when your affluent client agrees to personally introduce you, they will make this quite easy.

Also, this isn't just about connecting to other people through your clients; think in terms of arranging personal introductions from professional alliance partners and community spheres-of-influence as well. This is an ongoing part of Elite Advisors' business development efforts. They've honed the ability to uncover connections without being obvious. Then, they request introductions with simple and direct language. This isn't a one-off exercise; it's top of mind in every interaction with a client and a sphere-of-influence. "Who does this person know? How could they connect me?" Elite Advisors look at every relationship as the potential start of a snowball. This person has contacts; his contacts have contacts, etc.

ADVISOR EXERCISE: At our two-day live events, we have advisors perform a number of role-play exercises that typically pull them out of their comfort zones. One of these exercises requires the advisor to role-play calling a specific affluent client, asking to be introduced to a specific person within the client's spheres-of-influence.

Most participants are not yet experts at sourcing names, but every advisor knows a handful of people connected to their top clients—people they'd love to romance into becoming clients. So do you. So why don't you roll-up your sleeves and play along? Here's the challenge:

- Identify the name of an individual connected to a top client.
- Create a reason to call your client (i.e. follow-up from a recent meeting).
- Toward the end of your call, say something such as, "By the way, could you introduce me to Bill—that golfing buddy of yours? I'd like to meet him." (You've got an 83 percent chance of hearing "Sure" if you have a business *and* social relationship with the client).
- Before hanging up, tell your client that you'll check with him in a couple of days (specify a date and time) to see what works for Bill.

We challenge the advisors to make this call from their hotel rooms; setting up the introductions they've just role-played. When we do this, you'd think we just asked them to hand-feed a tank of hungry sharks. We know from experience, however, that if we can achieve some early "wins," we have an 87 percent chance of changing our participants' behavior, so we insist that they do this.

The homework results are consistent: 85 percent to 90 percent of the advisors have a personal introduction scheduled by the following morning. And when we ask what they learned, the answer is always the same: "It was easy."

None of this is complex. You simply need to interact with affluent clients and prospects in venues that you enjoy—at events where business isn't on the agenda. The secret: when business *does* come up in conversation, and it invariably does, discuss it briefly. Then, gently table that discussion, exchange cell phone numbers and set up a time and place for more detailed discussion. You then continue socializing. This is a skill that Elite Advisors have transformed into an art.

Indirectly Generated Referrals

The reputation of Elite Advisors precedes them. They are magnetic and as a result get more referrals than typical advisors. Specifically, they get more indirectly generated referrals, meaning referrals generated as a result of high-level, personalized service—not a lengthy referral spiel. Their clients are genuinely happy with the services, and are eager to share these feelings with friends, family and colleagues. This is where service links to marketing. High-level service puts advisors in a position to grow their businesses as it stimulates affluent "buzz"—word of mouth influence.

Social Network Analysis helps us understand the science behind word-of-mouth influence. This type of research goes back to the ancient Greeks, and today scientists are studying everything from relationships within high schools, to the spread of disease, to prostitution rings.

The classic plotting of a social network is a scattering of dots (nodes) connected by various lines (ties), forming a web of contacts. Smaller networks (friendships in a small neighborhood) can be drawn up rather quickly using pen and paper. If Phil and James are friends, they would be shown as two nodes tied together with a line.

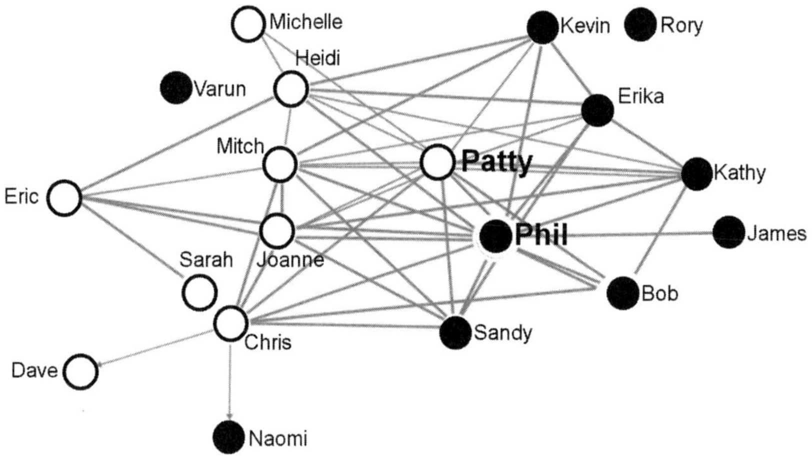

In the example above, notice the reach of a "Phil" or a "Patty." Chances are, if one needs a date, a quality CPA or even a good mechanic, they either know this person or have a friend who does. We find this fascinating as it relates to financial advisors and social prospecting.

Connected,[5] a book by Dr. Nicholas Christakis and James Fowler, offers an example of the role social networks play in marketing. They tell the story of two piano teachers in Arizona who grew their respective businesses through word-of-mouth. Neither of them advertised or promoted their services. At the end of the year, they analyzed their clientele and discovered that 38 percent of new business came by referral from people that hadn't personally used their services. These were referrals from friends and family of clients, who hadn't used their services personally, but had heard enough positive feedback to feel comfortable recommending this professional.

Whether you have twenty-five or 125 affluent clients, imagine the effect of word-of-mouth on your business. Every time you go the extra mile for your clients, take sincere interest in their well-being, or reach out with personal calls on their birthdays, there's a good chance they'll tell someone, that person will tell someone, and so on.

Often times, this conversation between your client and someone in their spheres-of-influence could result in the client giving out your contact information and recommending they give you a call. This is a great scenario, but you're not home free yet. The prospect still has to call you. What's more? Even if you get the prospect's contact information and begin calling them, it's often a futile effort. Months go by and you're often still trying to track this person down.

When an Elite Advisor is told by a client, "I gave your name to Mark Smith, a colleague at work. He should be calling you," the protocol is to thank the client and immediately transition the referral into a personal introduction. You can do this very easily by saying something like, "Thank you. I appreciate that. Why don't I take the two of you to lunch/dinner so you can personally introduce me? These things work best if we get to know each other before getting into business." Granted, it requires a couple of extra steps to set up the personal introduction, but it's the only way to go. Think about it. What are the odds of your client saying, "Sorry, I only give referrals. I don't do personal introductions?"

ADVISOR EXERCISE: If you're like most advisors, you've probably received some referrals from your clients over the past six months—people who were supposed to call but never did. You can resurrect these opportunities. You don't even need to remember the name of the referral—only the client.

Here's the drill: call your client, explain how you were never able to connect with the referral, and suggest that you treat them both to a lunch or dinner. Go for it. It works!

Not only is this a high-impact marketing activity, the odds are so well stacked in your favor (approximately 8 out of 10 clients will set up an introduction), that if this were Vegas, you'd be putting all your chips on the table.

Professional Alliances

Elite Advisors understand the power of professional alliances. With iron-clad alliances in place, they start each year fully expecting a handful of new ideal prospects to come their way—just from managing their professional relationships. It's been our experience that Elite Advisors typically have four to five good partners, not twenty or thirty, and they manage these relationships much like they do their top clients. Frequent interaction, both social and business, is their recipe for success. These CPAs, attorneys and other professional alliance partners are invited to lunch, dinner, client events and other social activities. They're also sent referrals when a client might need their services. This doesn't take as much time as you might think, but it does require a dedication to keeping this outside professional engaged throughout the year.

Many advisors think that sending referrals is the only element in the equation. When referrals aren't reciprocated, the advisor gets frustrated, determines that alliances with CPAs and attorneys don't work, and pays even less attention to these relationships. It's a vicious cycle.

Elite Advisors recognize the need for ongoing personal communication, socializing, and idea sharing. They also understand the value of accompanying their clients when referring them to a professional alliance partner.

A perfect example is how Mark, an advisor on a wealth management team, was able to develop a revenue sharing arrangement with a prestigious accounting firm. Our advisor knew one of the partners well enough, in his words, to "wave and say hello." His team had identified this CPA firm as a potential alliance partner. Mark took the initiative to call the CPA, suggesting they get together for a non-business lunch, just to get to know each other. That lunch led to dinner with their spouses and over the next six months there was ongoing social interaction with this CPA.

As their relationship evolved, trust developed to such a level that the CPA confided to Mark that he and his partners weren't really confident in their wealth management division. This accounting firm had brought on a financial advisor to handle investments. In the CPA's words, "We're comfortable with him handling clients in the $250,000 maybe up to the $1 million range, but definitely not when they get over the $1 million level."

Within a week of that conversation, six months after Mark took the initiative to develop a personal relationship with this CPA, the accounting firm agreed to refer clients at $1 million or greater to Mark's team as part of a signed revenue sharing agreement. Does it always happen like that? Of course not! Mark got lucky, but you can too if you engage in the right activities.

Effective alliances aren't always built on revenue sharing agreements. In fact, most have no official agreement at all. They're built purely for the sake of helping each professional drive new business and serve clients on a deeper level.

A case in point is Walter, an advisor in the Mid-Atlantic. Walter was working hard at developing a professional alliance with a CPA. He'd been taking this CPA to lunch for several months and even sent him six referrals, but it became apparent this was a one-way street. Walter could only think of one referral that had come from this CPA. Similar to Mark, Walter called this CPA and arranged a lunch, but this time business was clearly on the agenda.

During the lunch, Walter complimented the CPA on the tax work he'd been doing and then asked, "Just out of curiosity, is there a reason you haven't sent any referrals to me?" The CPA's response blew Walter away. He said, "I didn't think you needed referrals." The outcome was immediate; the CPA gave Walter a referral on the spot and promised that there was more to follow. This may seem too good to be true, but we've often found that by "regrouping" with alliance partners who haven't reciprocated, you're able to jump start these relationships.

Walter had done a decent job of managing the personal side of the relationship. He'd even sent six referrals to the CPA. The only "fly in the ointment" was they had never really talked about the structure of their relationship. Advisors often assume that CPAs and other professionals understand how these alliances are supposed to work. Many of them do not. As part of the ongoing relationship management process, there needs to be a time where advisor and alliance partner discuss the frequency of interaction, ideal client profile, referral process, areas of expertise, and so on.

Both Walter and Mark had a positive outcome in the examples we just shared, but we don't mean to imply that success is guaranteed. Far from it. It's still a numbers game and most likely you'll have to meet with a number of potential alliance partners before encountering the select few with whom you can develop a healthy relationship.

To jump start your professional alliance efforts, many of you might need to find a few new alliance partners. We suggest starting that process by going through your current connections. For the next 90 days, ask each client which other professionals they are using. Then ask them to rate these professionals on a 1 to 5 satisfaction scale. If they rate the professional a 5, you'd like to meet this person. If they rate them a 4, it's not a crisis, but you should give the client the option to be introduced to another professional. If they rate this professional a 3 or lower, strongly suggest that you set up a meeting with a professional who could serve them better.

It's also wise to ask your current professional alliance partners what other professionals they recommend. We're not saying to ask CPAs about other CPAs. That's probably not the smartest idea. But you can ask CPAs about attorneys and vice versa.

As soon as you identify a professional alliance partner with potential, you begin the process of getting to know them. Arrange an introductory lunch or coffee on the basis that you're both professionals in the same community or because you have a mutual client. At this point you're starting to profile them. Would they service your clients well? Do you get along with them? Do they understand how these relationships are supposed to work? Through ongoing contact you're able to filter out those professionals that aren't a good fit.

Your goal is to have a small group of alliance partners that you engage much like you would a top client. You communicate with them often and get to know them on a personal level, which strengthens the trust they have in you as a person.

We often find that advisors know very little about their professional alliance partners. They might know their area of expertise or the types of clients they service, but they don't know much about them on a personal level.

ADVISOR EXERCISE: At many of our workshops, we take advisors through a little exercise where they are to profile their professional alliance partners. They are to take out a sheet of paper, write down the name of a professional alliance, and begin listing everything they know about this person. This exercise doesn't take very long and you can probably guess why. Are you ready to take the challenge?

Profile 2-3 of your top professional alliance partners using the outline below:

- Name:
- Spouse's Name:
- Kids: Hobbies/Interests:
- Favorite Restaurants:
- College Attended:
- Favorite Sports Teams:

Would uncovering the answers to these questions strengthen your relationship with this professional? Would a stronger relationship lead to more business going back and forth? You bet it would.

Managing this relationship over the long term is the biggest challenge facing advisors with professional alliances. Many advisors are able to initiate the first contact, but find themselves challenged to remain in contact as the days and months wear on.

There are a number of paths you can take, both social and business, to keep these partners engaged. Although the objective is to develop a business relationship, it is important to remember that it is much easier to develop rapport on a social level. Why? Because everyone's defenses are down when socializing. This is why advisors should place more emphasis on social contacts for developing and strengthening referral alliance relationships.

This becomes easier as you get to know these professionals on a personal level. For instance, if you know any of their hobbies, sports, or recreational interests, you could organize a contact around that specific activity. If you know that a CPA and her spouse love to dine at a certain restaurant, you can suggest having dinner at this restaurant as couples.

The following is a partial list of tactics used by advisors to strengthen their relationship on a personal level:

- Invitation to small dinner party
- Invitation to holiday party
- Invitation to birthday party
- Dinner as couples
- Attending a local sporting event
- Playing golf
- Cycling
- Motorcycle riding
- Deep sea fishing / Fly fishing
- Organizing a weekly Captain's Choice golf outing
- Birthday dinner
- Hobbies / personal interest articles—emailed
- Birthday bottle of wine (spouse also)
- Volunteering on the same charitable committee
- Bottle of champagne on wedding anniversary
- Sports article relating to a child's high school sport
- Helping on a fundraiser for a personal cause

From a business perspective, generating ongoing contact can be in the form of:

- Meeting with client and financial organizer
- Participating in a client review meeting
- Invitation to an intimate breakfast with an economy / market update
- Invitation to an intimate client event
- Invitation to an intimate client event with opportunity to bring a client
- Email with pertinent PDF research attachment
- Coffee and bagels for office delivered during first week in April (CPAs)
- Deli sandwiches for office delivered during first week in April (CPAs)

- Calling about a potential client you'll be referring
- Meeting with potential client and professional partner
- Notification of a pertinent news item you've uncovered (email)

Both of these lists only scratch the surface of the options available. Our objective is to stimulate your creativity, and therefore increase your ability to orchestrate meaningful contact. In the next section on Intimate Client Events, you'll see how these are also a powerful vehicle for strengthening a professional alliance relationship.

Intimate Client Events

Large client events are a thing of the past, at least for an Elite Advisor. They're expensive, time consuming, and offer minimal time for relationship building. Smaller scale events that involve a handful of clients and guests (specific people sourced by the advisor) have become the event of choice for Elite Advisors. We refer to them as "intimate events" because that is precisely the objective—become intimate with affluent clients and prospects. The idea is to hold a small-scale social event that is fun, non-threatening, and a natural environment for strengthening relationships and developing rapport. In this manner, these events serve a dual purpose; they allow advisors to strengthen client relationships on a personal level and present an atmosphere that's conducive to personal introductions.

Elite Advisors have quickly become masters of intimate client events. They host regular events that their affluent clients and friends look forward to attending. The events involve husbands *and* wives whenever possible, and are typically small scale (six to twenty people in attendance). We've seen themes that range from wine tastings to skeet-shooting clinics and everything in between.

It isn't unusual for Elite Advisors to host monthly events throughout the year and to have these planned many months in advance. Scheduling them in advance ensures they are consistently held. There's a big difference in saying "we'll probably host a wine event in January and have another event February" versus saying "we have a wine event on January 27th and an economic update on February

23rd." Even with the best of intentions, January can turn into February, February can turn into March, and you're still planning your first event.

Done properly, these events involve a tremendous amount of preplanning. Elite Advisors (and their teams) make certain that the venue, food and drinks are up to par. They carefully plan their guest list and determine who they want each client to bring as a guest. They also do their homework; acquiring a bit of background information on every guest. When it's time for invitations, the advisor personally calls each client with an invite, making sure to properly "sell" the social nature of the event and the need to bring a specific guest. Personal involvement by the advisor ensures the right people are in attendance.

We've been teaching this tactic for over a decade and have had the pleasure of using this concept with some of the best advisors in the business. In doing so, we've seen phenomenal successes up close and personal. The following step-by-step guide is a synopsis of our research and experience on what works (and what doesn't) when it comes to the often mis-instructed area of client events.

1. Selecting the Right Clients

The first step in setting up an intimate client event is identifying the clients you would like to invite. This step is often skipped as many advisors want to start by selecting the event and picking a date—not so fast! Client event veterans build their events around their best clients, making certain their event will not only be appreciated, but stimulate positive word of mouth influence as well.

Your initial events should include those most likely to bring well-qualified guests. You want these events to build momentum, so you're basically setting the expectation in your first (or next) event that everyone brings a guest. All else equal, these will be some of your top clients because, more than likely, they associate with people of similar financial clout.

2. Selecting the Right Event

You want clients to bring guests, right? Then you need to select an event that's guest-worthy. If you pick something they consider boring (i.e. dinner event hosted by your firm), you won't entice them to invite anyone.

We are often asked what types of events are best. This is largely based on your specific client base, but we've seen the following events work well:

- Barbecues
- Sporting Events
- Cooking Classes
- Golf Clinics
- Art Gallery Events
- Private Museum Tours
- Cigar Night
- Tea Parties
- Fly Tying Class
- Hunting Trips
- Retirement Parties
- Birthday Parties
- Flower Arranging Class
- Holiday Parties
- Chocolate Tastings
- Ballroom Dance Classes
- Outdoor Concerts
- Theater Night
- Scotch Tastings
- Poker Night
- Tennis Clinics
- Tailgating
- Gardening Events
- Golf Simulator
- Spa Day
- Cake Decorating Class

3. The Invitation

The invitation is perhaps the most critical part of the whole client event process. Having the right people in attendance makes or breaks your events. We not only want clients and guests in attendance, we want your positioning to be strong, so the invitation has to send the right message.

The initial invitation needs to be done by phone (or in person). Sending a written invitation can serve as a nice secondary point of contact, but the initial invitation should only be handled by the advisor (not the assistant) either in person or over the phone.

The key points to emphasize in your introduction call are:

- This is an all fun, no business event
- Everyone is bringing a guest
- This is for a very small group of your best clients
- You will be calling back to confirm their attendance and to make note of the guest they plan to bring.

4. Pre-Event Planning

In preparation for the event, meet with your team (or assistant) to make certain that every detail of the event is in order. After all, you're hosting an event for your very best clients and their friends. The last thing you want is a poorly planned or poorly run event. It's the small things that make all the difference. The following are some important pre-event action items:

Plan for Client Coverage

Meet with your team (or assistant) to reinforce that no client or guest should be left alone. The critical times are the informal mingling time before the event and as everyone leaves. Plan to make certain everyone is receiving adequate attention at all times.

Gather Background Information

Make certain that you have gathered background information of each guest. If you haven't already, now is a good time to ask your clients about the person they are bringing. You can also conduct a quick Google and social media search on the person to see if they have any information listed on the web.

Plan for Follow-up

Elite Advisors are already brainstorming about follow-up opportunities before the first guest arrives. If you're able to arrange the follow-up at the event, it flows much more smoothly than calling people after you've parted ways. For instance, if you know that your client and her guest both enjoy the opera, look up some performances in the next month.

5. Conducting the Event

While you're at the event—it's showtime! Your only tasks are to build rapport, make certain everyone has a great time, and to generate some follow-up opportunities. The following are important points to remember:

- Make conversation with everyone in attendance, especially the guests. This is your time to build rapport and get to know everyone.
- Avoid the trap of talking too much and listening too little. Ask thoughtful questions of your guests and listen attentively to their answers.
- Bring a digital camera to take pictures of the event. It provides a great reason to follow-up with everyone afterwards.
- Be on the hunt for follow-up opportunities. This is critical. You want to find a way to follow-up with your clients' guests, without having to make it a sales call. Come into the event with several tracks already in mind for this purpose (i.e. round of golf, another client event you're holding, a ballgame, etc.). It will make it easier to naturally follow-up with people.
- Be prepared to mini-close. If someone is talking about the market or the economy or politics, offer a meeting to look things over. This situation will happen more often than you think, so be ready!

6. Event Follow-up

It should go without saying, but you *must* follow-up if you want to get new business from your client events. At this point, you've made this task fairly straightforward. You've already strengthened client loyalty with the clients who attended. Now it's time, if you haven't set up a next point of contact already, to set something up! Here are a few tips:

Promptly send the photographs you took at the event.

Attach a personal message to each e-mail to the client and/or prospect referencing the event and any surprise and delight information you uncovered about them. "Jim, thanks for coming, I know it's not like watching your Yankees play, but it looks like you (and your wife Julie, friend Joe, etc.) were having a great time in the third picture." Also, if you're holding an especially memorable event, you can go a step further and create a small photo album for guests.

Follow-up with a phone call to your client.

Within two or three days after the event, place a call to the clients that attended. This is mostly a "thanks for coming, we were honored by your presence" type of exchange. But it's also a good opportunity to ask them about the guest they brought. Did they enjoy themselves? Did they have any comments about the evening?

Follow-up with Guests

Hopefully, by the end of the event, you've got some follow-up opportunities in the works with each client's guest. If not, there's still time to follow-up afterwards:

1. Social—When you've identified some areas of commonality (sports fan, wine drinker, cyclist, etc.), your best bet is to follow-up socially. Invite them out to do something fun. An invitation to your next event is a great fallback option.
2. Business—When someone brings up business to you at the event, you should attempt to mini-close for an appointment. If you miss the mini-close opportunity at the event, you might call them and say something like: "I should have mentioned this Saturday, but we do a lot of work with (insert situation/topic they mentioned). You and I should probably get together and talk sometime early next week. Are you open for breakfast?"

It's not an overly complicated process, but it only works well for those who dedicate themselves to running effective events. We recognize that many advisors are hosting events nowadays, but not everyone is getting the results they seek. The following are the most common mistakes we see with advisors holding an intimate event, mistakes that keep them from getting the results enjoyed by Elite Advisors.

Common Intimate Event Mistakes

- They hold these events infrequently and therefore never get comfortable in the subtleties of hosting a small social event.
    - *Elite Advisors typically hold their intimate events on a monthly or bi-monthly basis and schedule them well in advance.*
- They spend less time in preparation, which involves selecting the right event for the right clients.
    - *Elite Advisors have invested the time to know what their affluent clients enjoy and craft their events accordingly.*
- They take shortcuts in the invite process; instead of making a personal call, they delegate this task to an assistant, some even use email.
    - *Elite Advisors personally invite their clients and "sell" the event as a true non-business, fun event.*
- They ask their clients to bring a guest, but haven't sourced a name and asked for a specific guest to attend.
    - *Elite Advisors have sourced names within their client's spheres-of-influence and ask for that specific couple (sourced name) to attend.*
- They don't do homework on the guests who are attending, which places them at a disadvantage for following-up.
    - *Elite Advisors know the names of everyone who will be attending, and Google search, etc., to gather information about each*

guest that will assist both in developing rapport and following-up.

- They lack a game plan, which we refer to as "strategic intent."
    - *Elite Advisors have a game plan for each client, whether it's sourcing another name, developing a better relationship with a spouse, or connecting with a client guest. Usually it's all of the above.*
- No follow-up.
    - *Elite Advisors have a game plan, they always follow-up with both clients and guests.*

What's important for advisors to understand is that the more emphasis placed on the fact that these are non-business "fun" events, the more business will result. This is counterintuitive. Today's affluent don't like sales people and don't like their advisor pushing their services on people they know, and yet, when the environment is non-threatening, it becomes safe to initiate a business conversation.

Remember the power of word-of-mouth influence and getting personally introduced. This is the #1 manner in which today's affluent discovered their current financial advisor. Year after year, our data reveals that intimate events and other social venues are the foundation of an Elite Advisor's marketing plan.

We've talked about the activity component of this—be active socially, host intimate events, etc., but now we're going to shift focus to the skill component. Many advisors have the right social connections, but heretofore haven't been able to convert them to business prospects. The following section will teach you this ever-important skill for driving new business in social venues.

Social Prospecting

In today's environment, social prospecting is what cold calling was 25 years ago. It's what seminars were 15 years ago. Today's affluent are fearful of doing business with anyone they haven't gotten to know and trust. This is why social prospecting works among the affluent, and why cold calling and seminars are less and less effective.

When asked, "What's your biggest challenge with social prospecting?" advisors participating in our recent survey reported that the two biggest issues were, "Not wanting to appear salesy" and "Not having wealthy social contacts."[6] We've seen this play out in the industry for years. Why? In many ways, the affluent can be intimidating. Industry-wide, even when an advisor has the right connections, the conversion from social contact to a business prospect isn't happening very frequently.

For most, this is a mind game—the fear of coming across salesy or being rejected. We've coached many advisors into heavy social prospecting campaigns. We would know if they were ruining their social relationships. This is hardly the case. When we coax advisors to become more active with social prospecting, their response is usually, "I should have been doing this a long time ago!"

Armed with the knowledge that most affluent investors are dissatisfied enough to change advisors, Elite Advisors consistently put themselves in positions where they meet wealthy people, develop rapport with them, and earn the right to compete for their business.

Whenever they're in these social environments (charity functions, kids' sporting events, etc.), which is often, their antennas are activated for conversations (opportunities) to make a well-placed comment that will turn a social contact into a business prospect.

We refer to this artful marketing tactic as the "re-direct." As the name implies, the re-direct involves steering conversations about the economy, a specific stock, a life event or any other related topic into conversations about what you're experiencing with your clients and, ultimately, into a conversation about what you could do for this social contact.

When faced with a political or financial conversation, many advisors fall into the trap of talking too much. They're passionate about politics, knowledgeable about investments, and use these conversations as an opportunity to showcase their smarts. More often than not, this becomes a circular conversation, ending with the advisor in no better position to sell than when the conversation began. Even worse, the investment-focused conversation positions the advisor as salesy, even without explicitly pitching his or her wares.

We recommend cutting these conversations short by redirecting this social contact into a more productive discussion. This requires shifting gears quickly and seamlessly, which requires practice. Here's how we frame it in a 4-step process:

Scenario: Prospect is commenting, or even venting, about something related to politics, the economy or the markets.

1) Allow the prospect to conclude his or her stream of consciousness.
2) Acknowledge without agreeing: "I hear you . . ." "I understand . . ."—repeating a portion of their stream of consciousness.
3) Re-direct: "With all that's going on with (stay topical), I'm amazed how few people with means have had a risk analysis conducted on their family's finances." Or you might say, "That's why we've been working so closely with our clients making sure they're protected from all of this—and looking for any opportunities we can find."
4) Read the prospect. If you've got their attention, offer a second opinion (mini-close). "We should probably get together . . ."

There's no magic script for redirecting conversations. The secret is practicing your language, not ours, over and over until it becomes second nature. The more you rehearse, the more easily the language rolls off your tongue, even in the stickiest of social situations. With the right language, you can sell to anyone, anywhere. Even though you might feel silly at first, practice your language in front of the mirror, in your car, with your spouse, etc. It will start the process of speaking fluent rainmaker.

The reason for this tactic's effectiveness is simple: affluent investors have been shaken up by the volatility in the markets, they want to minimize risk, and their current financial advisor probably isn't addressing their concerns. Therefore, they need a *trusted* financial professional to oversee their financial affairs, not an opinionated know-it-all who talks too much.

Essentially, you're respectfully gaining control of the conversation, getting the attention of the person who's been talking, and subtly offering your services—almost as a favor.

Here's a key point: the less you talk, the better your results. Sure, you're offering your services, but you're not explaining any details of what you do. Too many advisors cheapen the meeting by going into too much detail about what they want to talk about, including areas of expertise. As a result, they don't actually get the meeting. If they ask, simply respond, "It's very involved. I'll walk you through it personally" and continue to close for the appointment.

Affluent prospects are very reluctant to turn over their family's finances to an advisor they don't yet know or trust on a personal level. This is why social prospecting is so powerful. It's 95 percent about managing relationships and 5 percent about selling. Elite Advisors recognize re-direct opportunities and take action.

ADVISOR EXERCISE: You might be thinking, "Where was this information a few months ago?!? I could have used it on the golf course when XYZ prospect was talking with me about XYZ topic." Have no fear; you can still revisit those situations. We recommend running the following drill:

Think Back. Jog your memory over the past six weeks to when you've been in a conversation about a certain stock, the market as a whole or any other financial topic. Nearly all of these conversations, even if you didn't seize the opportunity at the time, can be revisited.

Create a List. Make note of missed opportunities from the past six weeks that includes:

- The name of the person with whom you were speaking.
- The topic discussed.
- The time/place you will re-approach them.

The Right Language. We recommend saying something such as, "A while back, you had some questions about XYZ. I should have offered this back then, but I'd like to sit down with you and talk further about what you're doing financially."

This might be the quickest way to repay your investment in this book. We often find that advisors can think of four to six examples within a few minutes.

BEWARE!! Top Five Ways Advisors Appear Salesy

We've seen many advisors who weren't willing to socially prospect. They considered friends, family members and committee members off limits. This is a "common cold" mindset afflicting many advisors.

In reality, most advisors are miles away from the "used car salesman" persona they fear. It's been our experience that advisors who are overly fearful of being salesy wouldn't come across salesy if they tried. It's like the guy going to the gym for the first time and telling his trainer that he doesn't want to get too muscular. It's not going to happen.

Most advisors should be more assertive when offering their services to social contacts. For that to happen, they must get over the fear of being perceived as salesy. Sales are part of the job and, besides, you probably do great work. You have to believe that, by offering your services to them, you're doing social contacts a big favor.

Let's review some of the main ways in which advisors come across as salesy. We think you'll find that most of these attributes are easily avoided.

1) **Talking too much.**
   This usually takes the form of talking about what you do, how much you know, and how good you are. When you try too hard to make a good first impression, it usually backfires. It comes across as self-absorbed bragging, and it is salesy. From the newest rookie to the most grizzled veteran, everyone claims to be good at their craft—fully capable of serving the needs of the affluent. In social settings, talking too much about your ap-

proach, your team and your experience is a guaranteed "prospect repellent."

2) **Sales before Relationship.**
This is a relationship business. Approaching someone about handling their finances before letting them get to know you on a personal level reeks of "pushy salesman." An insurance agent came to our office recently to meet with one of our associates. Before he made it down the hall, he introduced himself to one of our coaches, told him all about his firm and expertise, and tried to schedule a meeting. Sales alert! Next time he sees this person coming, our coach will close his office door.

3) **Being Too Scripted.**
This industry gets a fair amount of sales training—some good; a lot of it "old school." The focus on value propositions is a perfect example of antiquated salesmanship. Someone poses the "What do you do?" question at a social event, and the response is delivered as if some "play button" was just pressed. Invariably, the response is too long, too descriptive (with too much industry jargon), and comes across as disingenuous. This activates a sales alert in the prospect's mind. The affluent instantly detect and disregard scripted, salesy language.

4) **Handing out Business Cards.**
As innocent as this might seem, prematurely handing out business cards is old school, and in today's environment it's a turn-off. Handing out brochures is even worse. Why? Because the affluent perceive them as a sales piece, not as a helpful document that explains your services. We've also seen advisors adopt the practice of not carrying business cards, but we don't recommend this, because it gives the wrong impression if you receive a sincere request for your card. If asked, exchange cards, but be sure to exchange cell phone numbers as well.

5) **Pushy Follow-up.**
We've all experienced overly aggressive follow-up. Some salespeople are much too obvious. You meet the person once, and he

> tries to immediately set up an appointment to pitch his wares. He calls too many times, sends too many emails, and has as much finesse as an M-1 Abrams tank driving through a gift shop. Follow-up is an art. Too little or too much can spell disaster.
>
> You're *not* being salesy if you ask someone to discuss business. It's part of your role as a stand-up professional, a community steward and a go-to financial coordinator for the affluent. You owe it to yourself to offer your services when the right situation is presented.
>
> Think of sales as shooting a basketball. If you shoot five free throws and they're all hitting the front of the rim, you'd give the next shot some extra oomph, and get the ball to the back of the rim. You're overcorrecting as a means to finding the sweet spot. The same holds true for social prospecting. If you find yourself failing to ask for the business (shooting short), you need to be a little more assertive. You might feel like you're pushing the envelope, but in reality, it's probably just the right amount. Whether it's foul shooting or social prospecting, you've got to be *in the game* to improve your game.

From a business development perspective, the focus of Elite Advisors has changed dramatically. Standard sales tactics (cold calling, direct mail, public seminars) no longer work with today's affluent. Trust is so fragile with the affluent and they're so guarded against being sold that affluent sales and marketing tactics have taken a new form. The proverbial business line of "features and benefits" has metamorphosed into a personal form. Now the advisor is the product; "features and benefits" has become very personal.

Financial advisors need to become skilled in the art of social prospecting in affluent circles. As we've indicated throughout this chapter, it's easier to develop rapport and let people feel as though they're getting to know you when there are no business barriers in the way. Which is why the less business advisors discuss in social settings, the more business they're likely to obtain. Elite Advisors understand this and have become masters of the "less is more" philosophy. Less talking, more impact. Less business talk, more business. Less industry jargon, more sincerity, and so on.

None of this is very complicated. Affluent sales and marketing is actually a simple process for any advisor who is willing to get personal and take the initiative to master the art of selling in affluent circles. Simple, yes, but easy, no. You might want to think of it as back to basics with a 21st century Great Recession influence. Asking to be introduced to a friend or colleague of a loyal client isn't very difficult. But you must have loyal affluent clients. It's the essence of relationship management. When it's lacking, relationship marketing in affluent circles is nearly impossible.

Key Takeaways

- A personal introduction is the #1 manner that today's affluent investor first discovered their financial advisor.
- 83 percent of affluent clients will introduce their advisor if they have a business and social relationship with the advisor, 66 percent will introduce their advisor if the relationship is business only.
- The #1 event an affluent client will attend is an intimate "fun" event. It is also the #1 event to which they'll bring a guest.
- Very few financial advisors are taking advantage of the business development opportunities created by the Great Recession. Only a small fraction of advisors are acquiring 5 or more $1 million plus new relationships a year.
- Word-of-mouth influence in affluent spheres-of-influence has a major impact on discovering and selecting a financial advisor.
- Successful marketing activities require personal interaction; strategic networking, introductions, professional alliances, and intimate events.
- Elite Advisors excel at sourcing (uncovering) names within their affluent client's spheres-of-influence.
- Advisors should strive to source 3-4 names a week; think in terms of the affluent client's 7 spheres-of-influence.
- Treat referral alliance partners like top clients. Develop a personal relationship with referral alliance partners and you will receive more referrals.
- *The Relationship Management / Relationship Marketing Nexus™* is all about getting social with clients, prospects and professional alliance partners.

4

Client Loyalty

Factoid: 54% of affluent women say their financial advisor is a great problem solver.[1]

Taylor was meeting with one of his top client families. He was very proud of himself, as this client's $5 million portfolio was up eighteen percent over the past year. During the review, Taylor carefully explained to this husband and wife his investment philosophy and his game plan for the upcoming year. Then he concluded by asking if either of them had any questions. They had none, and the review ended on a cordial and professional note as Taylor escorted them to the elevator. Two weeks later, Taylor received a call from the husband: "I've got some bad news. My wife is taking out $4 million because she has a financial planner she wants to use."

As Taylor relayed this story six weeks later, it was obvious that he was still in a state of disbelief. He couldn't fathom that "after earning $900,000 on their portfolio, the wife moves eighty percent of the money to a planner!" Only after a lengthy discussion did Taylor realize that he was never connecting with the wife. His relationship was with the husband, who was pleased with the eighteen percent return. But he didn't understand the female of this affluent household. As it turned out, she was far more risk-averse than her husband, but she didn't feel the need to interrupt Taylor's soliloquy. Behind the scenes, however, she expressed herself *very* clearly to her husband, "do you think we could lose it as fast as we made it?"

Lessons Learned:

- Talking isn't communicating. Taylor talked about his investment acumen throughout the review, failing to create an environment in which his clients (husband and wife) felt comfortable expressing their true feelings.
- Financial planning and risk management are critical issues for today's affluent; for women even more so than men.
- Today's affluent don't give their financial advisor credit for their portfolio being up when the markets are also up.
- The affluent female of the household is the key to strengthening the relationship.

Investment performance alone doesn't create loyalty. You must also provide a high level of personalized service and be proactive with communication. It's hard work, but well worth the effort. Loyal affluent clients are an Elite Advisor's acre of diamonds. They will entertain new ideas that you present, allowing you to reposition (rebrand) the scope of services that you offer, and they will take you into their spheres-of-influence, making them a key ingredient in any marketing plan. Once again, this is *The Relationship Management / Relationship Marketing Nexus*™ at work.

Loyalty is built through relationship management of both spouses. This requires a blend of professionalism (personalized Ritz Carlton-quality service with FedEx-level efficiency), surprise and delight (thoughtful gifts and gestures), and well planned social interactions. Advisors need to raise the bar—to offer this type of attention to the *entire* affluent client unit.

A strong case can be made that it's becoming an affluent woman's world, and this goes beyond the fact that women outlive men. Today's affluent women are taking a more active role in every aspect of their family's finances. We've labeled this the Affluent Gender Shift.

The Affluent Gender Shift

1. Affluent women place more importance than men on most of the criteria ranked as important regarding their financial advisor relationship.[3]
2. The recent financial crisis has forced conversations between husband and wife on protecting family assets and maintaining lifestyles—both now and in retirement.
3. Affluent women are more educated, financially literate and involved than ever before.

We understand that it's easier to maintain the status quo, but this initiative is good for the client (*both* should be involved in making financial decisions) and good for the advisor (you're strengthening the relationship and opening another door for COI penetration). In fact, the non-participating spouse may be the person who manages the family's social calendar.

Client Profiling

"Every battle is won before it is ever fought," wrote the Chinese general Sun-Tzu in 500 BC in *The Art of War*. This book is still influential today, not only in military planning but in business and other competitive endeavors. What does this quote mean, and how does it apply to a financial professional? Sun-Tzu is telling you that preparation is the key to winning any battle.

As you battle for the hearts, minds and wallets of your best prospects and clients, keep in mind that intelligence-gathering is one of the most valuable tools at your disposal. The most successful financial advisors transform their financial practices into intelligence-gathering practices as well.

Managing relationships with top affluent clients is a fairly straightforward concept. Your goal is to interact with clients on both a professional and personal level. Most advisors understand the professional nature of the relationship—in-person annual reviews, effective practice management, problem solving, personal communication, proactive financial advice, and so on. However it's the personal aspect of the relationship that tends to be more challenging. If you're just getting started with your "getting personal" initiative, start discussing things like your clients' family, hobbies, favorite sports teams and vacations. The more you get to know them, the more they get to know you, and the more they trust and want to help you.

You want to enlist the services of everyone on your team to help personalize every client relationship. This can be as simple as empowering support personnel to engage affluent clients with personal questions about hobbies, family or upcoming events. For instance, an affluent client calls with questions about a recent statement and, after resolving the problem, the team member asks, "So, when do the kids get out of school?" or "How's your daughter's soccer team doing?" The nature of the question doesn't matter as much as the personal and sincere nature of the questioner. It's important to remember that affluent clients want you to know them on a personal level. This is a team effort.

Speaking of a team effort, the following is a sampling of the type of information Elite Advisors gather on affluent clients. The idea is for everyone on your team to participate in uncovering this information. The more you know, the easier it is to strengthen loyalty.

Affluent Client Profile:

- Name
- Marital status
- Spouse's name
- Home address
- Vacation home address
- Wedding anniversary
- Hometown
- Hometown (spouse)
- Birth dates
- College(s) & graduation date(s)
- Military service
- Business
- Business address
- Position
- Spouse business
- Business address
- Position
- Previous employment
- Children (their names, status, etc.)
- Grandchildren
- Health issues or history
- Community activities

Political activities
Religious activities
Service organizations
Favorite restaurants
Hobbies, sports, recreational interests
Vacation habits
Cars driven
Conversational habits
Close friends
Close family

*Note—This information should be gathered over time through conversation. It is far less impactful to gather this information through survey.

Relationship Management Tactics

Relationship-building can be achieved through a simple phone call, but this process works best face-to-face. We've found that many clients love getting together "just to catch-up." All sorts of information can surface during these social encounters—from names that will lead to introductions to relationship-strengthening "surprise and delight" opportunities. Much can be gained by devoting the right amount of energy to the right clients.

Like so much in life, an advisor's mindset is the key to effective relationship management. It's not that advisors don't recognize the importance of managing relationships with affluent clients. They do. The problem is that their perception of relationship management revolves around business. "If I'm not discussing business, what do I talk about?" is a question we often hear from advisors. We've also heard that advisors often feel guilty whenever they are out of the office in some non-business venue with a client. And their staff feeds the guilt by making remarks such as, "It must be nice having a two-hour client lunch."

Fortunately, the guilt dissipates once advisors discover the value of non-business engagements. They learn that whenever the venue is officially "non-business," defenses come down, personal issues surface, and business usually comes up in some fashion.

The following are some core tactics we've seen Elite Advisors use to develop stronger personal relationships with affluent clients. The activities are simple, but require discipline to do them consistently. Consistent execution is what enables Elite Advisors to hone their social skills.

Non-Business Lunches

This is not a new concept, but too many advisors have fallen into the habit of eating lunch by themselves or with other advisors. Because they view this as an important aspect of their business, Elite Advisors set aside certain days of the week for entertaining client couples over lunch. They treat these outings as scheduled events, even though they're one-on-one. This adds structure to their "getting personal" campaigns, ensuring that they meet regularly with top clients. These have been referred to as "Power Lunches"—a term referring to a lunch with the right people (top clients, prospects or COIs) at the right venues (a restaurant or social club that attracts the power players).

Points to Remember:

- Schedule lunches with clients two to four weeks in advance. This ensures that your calendar stays full and that you can get on busy clients' schedules.
- Dinners can work as well, but be mindful of the client's work and family situation when suggesting times and days of the week. A family with young children will have trouble with a mid-week dinner—just as a surgeon might have trouble breaking for lunch.
- You always want to approach each non-business lunch with strategic intent (a game plan). It could be to expand a relationship with a spouse, to uncover names within their spheres-of-influence or to ask for a personal introduction.
- Gather intelligence about your clients' favorite restaurants, and suggest these places when inviting them to lunch.
- Prepare for the lunches by reviewing the personal information you've gathered about these clients.

- Be willing to share personal information about yourself. This increases what your clients will share in return.
- Post-lunch, remember to document any new information you uncovered about family developments, changes at work, etc.
- Post-lunch, send a handwritten note with a personal message such as, "It was great to catch-up. I'm sure Amy will do very well in her new job."

Intimate Client Events

Intimate Client Events play an important role in getting social with your clients. These events provide a natural forum for socializing with a handful of affluent clients at the same time. They also allow clients to get to know you and your team on a more personal level.

As you'll recall from the Business Development Chapter, the primary reason for hosting these events is to build loyalty with *existing* affluent clients. This means you shouldn't spend all of your time talking with prospects and clients' guests. An advisor recently told us about a conversation he had with a client after holding an intimate wine tasting. The advisor called the client about an unrelated issue and asked, "Did you enjoy the wine event?" She replied, "Well, it was OK, but I must say I was a bit hurt that you barely spoke to me at the event. You must have had more important people to talk to." Ouch. This was one of his best clients. The point was well taken: the primary focus of client events is to build *client* loyalty.

With that in mind, keep the guest list to fewer than twenty people (ideally, ten to twelve). The idea is to initiate meaningful conversations with everyone in attendance—clients and guests. Wine tastings, minor league games and other mingle-friendly events are best because you have the chance to mill around and talk with everyone.

Before the event, develop specific discussion points linked to each client. By doing your homework in advance and then engaging clients in discussions about their hobbies and interests, you're getting personal and showing them you really care. Because of this, they're likely to return to future events.

Points to Remember:

- Select events that involve both spouses and appeal to a variety of interests. Hosting only golf, fishing and sporting events will likely alienate one spouse or the other.
- Invite a manageable number of guests—no more than twenty. This ensures you have time to mingle and engage each person in meaningful conversation.
- Create a game plan with your team to make sure every client gets adequate contact.
- Personally invite clients by telephone and emphasize all-fun and no-business.
- Host events on a monthly basis. If they're set up properly, they will be affordable and simple logistically.
- Schedule your events well in advance. We find that planning events three to six months in advance increases the number of events conducted throughout the year.
- Follow up with each client personally and discuss the event and how glad you were to see them.

Personal Phone Calls

The affluent have a preference for face-to-face contact, but phone calls and emails can also help in relationship-building. This personal call can take many forms—birthday calls, anniversary calls, holiday calls, catching-up calls and so on. Your personal phone call campaign should target both spouses even if, and especially if, one of the spouses isn't as actively involved in the family's finances. Whenever you call the less active spouse, frame the call along the lines of, "How are you? I don't get to chat with you as often. Is there anything on your mind financially?"

It also helps to empower all of your team members to get personal, suggesting conversations they can have and questions they can ask. A little scripting goes a long way.

Remember, this campaign *must* be personal. Elite Advisors pay attention to the contact preferences of their top clients. Some may want communication weekly, while others will prefer less frequent contact, and would be annoyed if you're always "checking in."

Points to Remember:

- Keep both spouses in the call rotation.
- Call top clients around birthdays and holidays. This is much more personal than email, and will complement any physical cards you might send.
- You can actually "hear" a smile through the phone. You might even want to stand up. It gives you more energy and enthusiasm.
- Script your team on questions to ask. "Do you have plans for the upcoming holiday? How are the kids?" Etc.
- Document any information you uncover. Each call can uncover a treasure trove of personal information.

Building Relationships Online

Since more of the affluent are joining social networking sites, it's important to engage in online conversations. But it must be done properly. The objective isn't to build your network just so you can post economic updates and thoughts on the markets. That will negatively affect your ability to establish personal relationships. Instead, use the information you gather from clients and COIs to spark offline conversations around their interests, backgrounds or connections.

The first step is connecting with clients on LinkedIn and Facebook. Facebook is especially important when it comes to getting personal, as you're sharing photos, personal events and other non-business information. If need be, create a separate "list" within Facebook that limits clients' ability to see certain pictures and posts you might not want them to see. Then, take a few minutes prior to your meetings to profile clients online.

Points to Remember:

- Social media can enhance, not replace, your client service and marketing initiatives.
- LinkedIn is the most popular medium for advisors to interact

with clients. It has a wealthy user-base and attracts more professionals and business owners than other social networking sites.

- Seek out both spouses online. Many times, if one spouse has an account, the other does, too.
- Be careful with your online reputation. Connecting with questionable characters who post inappropriate material or engage in offensive behavior can damage your reputation.
- Treat social media as a fluid, ongoing campaign, not as a one-off effort to "go digital."

Surprise and Delight

One of the best ways to show that you're really listening is to "surprise and delight" your affluent clients. Some refer to this as "Wowing," but we think "surprise and delight" is more descriptive because that's exactly the intention. Surprise and delight can be accomplished with any thoughtful gesture. It could be a small gift such as a Rick Steve's travel guide if you discover a client is taking a vacation in Europe. It could be a newspaper clipping when someone's grandchild makes the newspaper. It could be an order of soup if they have a sick family member. All of these personal touches tend to come as surprises to clients and they are delighted at the thoughtfulness, which is why it works wonders for warming up client relationships. You're showcasing that you really *do* care about your client on a personal level.

We hear stories of surprise and delight at nearly every workshop we conduct. Jim, a coaching client of The Oechsli Institute, recently shared a personal success story with us. During a meeting with one of his clients, a retired physician, he asked about the client's summer plans. The client mentioned he was going to take a golfing trip to Myrtle Beach, S.C. Jim asked with whom he was going and how he knew those individuals.

It became apparent the trip was hastily planned. Realizing this, Jim purchased a $15 golf course guide to Myrtle Beach and hand-delivered it to his client a few days before the trip. It turns out the guide came in very handy and the physician couldn't thank Jim enough.

Weeks later, the physician invited Jim to play golf with a couple of the same friends who'd gone on the trip with him—also retired physicians and ideal prospects. In the end, a $15 book turned into two personal introductions simply because Jim had been listening.

Another one of our coaching clients, Larry, shared another example. One of his clients had recently moved into an assisted living facility. When Larry asked how she was adjusting, she said it was OK, but she really missed her garden. She'd been growing tomatoes, herbs and other vegetables most of her life.

The next week, Larry went out and bought a potted tomato plant and a mini herb garden and delivered it to her room. In the words of Larry, "She couldn't stop thanking me!" Two months later she moved an account from her "broker" at another firm. She's now one of Larry's largest clients.

The point of this is not the immediate gratification of getting a new account or being introduced. It's all about client service and showing that you care. The additional business is just a nice side effect. Most advisors do something nice like this for a client . . . every now and then. Elite Advisors weave the concept of surprise and delight into the fabric of their business. Because these advisors and support personnel are on a mission to learn more about their clients, their antennas are always up for major life events, vacations, hobbies, etc.

Points to Remember:

- Enlist the help of your support personnel. They typically get excited about this initiative, and are a great source of ideas. Plus, you want them to be involved in the necessary fact finding. Hint—surprise and delight your team members first. It's a great way to showcase how this concept works.
- Be personal. A sleeve of golf balls isn't nearly as personal as an article clipping. A company-branded mini-cooler isn't as powerful as an outfit for their new grandchild.
- Think *inexpensive.* The more you spend, the more you raise suspicions about your intentions.
- Catalog your best ideas. Having a few places you frequent for

small gifts (Amazon.com, XYZ bakery, wine.com, etc.) makes the logistics far easier.

Final Thoughts on Loyalty

It is important to translate all of the common-sense advice in this chapter into common practice. The time and attention advisors devote to truly understanding affluent clients, as well as letting affluent clients get to know them, is priceless.

Elite Advisors realize that an affluent clientele is their "acre of diamonds." Not only do these clients generate a lion's share of the annual revenue stream, they are an integral part of the business development strategy. Here is today's reality: if an affluent client likes and respects you on a professional level, and if you've developed a business *and* personal relationship, 83 percent of the time you ask to meet someone within that client's sphere-of-influence, he or she will be happy to facilitate the meet and greet. That is a powerful marketing tactic.

Recently, the senior partner of a team with over $3 billion in assets explained his epiphany:

> *"I've got non-business lunches booked solid for the next two months. And I've got to admit, I had no idea how powerful these lunches would be. First of all, I had to overcome my guilt of not being in the office, and get everyone off my back for being out on these two-hour lunches. This became easy once I realized how much business I was conducting during these non-business lunches. I'm uncovering money as if it's falling from trees. Half the time, I don't even need to source names since my clients are suggesting people who should be doing business with me. Heck, we then spend the rest of the lunch brainstorming the venue for a personal introduction. This has been great! I've been rejuvenated. Been in the business for over 30 years, and I've never had so much fun."*

In the spirit of complete self-awareness, this Elite Advisor confessed that 25 years ago, these were the tactics that he and his partner used to build such a successful business. They were so successful that their firm had them traveling the country to tell advisors the story, and they did this to such an extent that they veered away from what made them successful.

None of this is complicated, but it can't be mechanically induced. It's upfront and personal. It's one affluent client, one affluent prospect, one referral alliance partner, one intimate event, one personal lunch, one surprise and delight at a time—over time.

Key Takeaways:

- Investment performance is important, but getting to know clients personally is the key ingredient in building loyalty.
- Elite Advisors put structure around relationship management. They have a plan for client lunches, surprise and delight, and other relationship-building tactics.
- Intimate Client Events are a great way to strengthen the loyalty of your affluent clients.
- Each team member plays a role in affluent loyalty. Your support personnel should have hands-on training (by you) regarding the level of service expected and the types of information that can be gathered during meetings and phone calls.
- Analyze the contact you're having with husband and wife, business-wise and socially, for each of your top affluent clients. This is a yearly exercise that needs to be conducted.

5

Practice Management

Factoid: 57% of financial advisors either share an assistant or don't have an assistant.[4]

"We lost a client. Nearly lost two," said Jack during a recent coaching call. "This is so frustrating. We're finally starting to bring in new business, but we can't be losing business out the backdoor at the same time."

The tipping point was a conversation with one of their wealthiest clients. Year after year, they had taken this client out for her birthday. She was a widow and had very little family, so this annual lunch was the highlight of her birthday.

For a variety of reasons, they forgot about the lunch this year.

Three days later, she called their office and said something along the lines of, "I was really hurt when I didn't get a call about my birthday lunch this year. I know you're busy, but …"

After reviewing the client's notes, Jack realized that, in addition to the missed birthday, he hadn't met with her in nearly eight months. This was hardly the high level service that his team had promised. Something had to change. Their service had become reactive at best, and was in danger of igniting an advisor's worst nightmare—negative word-of-mouth influence. Jack's team has become operationally inefficient.

Operational efficiency is like preventive medicine: it reduces the odds that surgical intervention will be needed to resolve serious problems. Jack's team was in the ER waiting room. Like many wealth management teams, they'd taken their affluent clients for granted. And because they assumed their services were up to par, they focused all their attention on "filling the bucket." They didn't realize that the bucket was full of holes until the birthday debacle.

Marketing is a key component of every Elite Advisor's practice. However, this particular team had fallen into a marketing-compulsion trap—one that created a lethal mix of practice-management issues:

- Too many smaller clients.
- Reactive client process with no clear and consistent service models.
- Blurry roles and responsibilities among support personnel, creating strained relationships.
- Sparse internal communication and few (if any) team meetings.
- Less communication with affluent clients.
- Lack of personalized service for affluent clients.

The loss of this good client was the team's wake-up call. To Jack's credit, his team made a concerted effort to improve each of the areas listed above. They recognized that it was time to start running their firm like a high-level professional business. A serious commitment to client segmentation was a top priority, followed by creating clear service models that would be understood and followed by everyone on the team. This set the stage for redefining individual roles, areas of responsibilities and the associated tasks.

At this juncture, Jack realized that the only way to open the channels of communication within the team was to make weekly team meetings a priority. This also allowed him to inspect what he expected from each individual. In addition to meetings, they began holding daily huddles at the start of each day—just to review the upcoming day.

From the vantage point of affluent clients, the results were immediate: better service, more communication from the team and more personalized communication. Fast-forwarding nine months, they've improved in all areas. By their own admission, they are "far from perfect," but they *have* implemented all of the basic practice-management procedures. These procedures will enable them to strengthen the relationships with their current affluent clients while acquiring new affluent clients from word-of-mouth influence.

Jack is one of many practice management revivals we've seen over the years; we've been writing a newsletter on this topic for ten years running. With so many potential practice management topics, we decided to narrow the focus of this chapter to a handful of key areas—areas with the most impact on strengthening relationships with existing affluent clients and freeing you up to find new affluent clients:

- Managing your inventory (client base).
- Segmenting your client base.
- Creating service models.
- Working more efficiently with support staff.
- Conducting effective team meetings.

Put your *Harvard Business Review* cap on, and get ready to make a few notes. We know you're always looking to refine your operations.

Managing Your Inventory

Inventory usually elicits thoughts of inanimate objects—digital watches, tubes of toothpaste, clothing, automobiles, and so on. As a financial advisor, your inventory is alive and breathing. It's your client base. Too much inventory, in a product or a service business, creates obstacles to operational efficiency.

Let's take a look at a product-focused example, which provides some great insights for the service industry. In a product-focused business, having too much inventory means tying up money in unproductive assets, paying for excess storage, risking spoilage, and so on. The following article by Microsoft and Dionco Inc. provides a great illustration:

> **The Real Cost of Inventory**[7]
> It is a fact that for almost all retailers inventory is the single largest asset on the balance sheet. Yet, despite all the improvements in technology over the past 25 years, inventory continues to be the least productive asset for most retailers.

> To determine inventory productivity we use a measure called "turnover" which tells us how many times inventory sells out in a year. In almost every segment of specialty retail—gift, clothing, sporting goods, jewelry, shoes, books, music, electronics, appliances, furniture, and many more—the stock turnover rates have held steady for over 25 years in the under 4 range and in a few cases, at less than 2 turns per year.
>
> This means that for most of these stores they are carrying at least three months of sales in their store at any given moment, and in the case of books and some other categories, the inventory approaches a six month supply at most times. This amount of inventory is not only a drain on the stores' financial position, but it also often reduces customer service because in most cases the store cannot afford to re-stock what is selling because they have too much of what is not selling.
>
> Clearly, retailers need to take a step back and critically address this problem and begin to manage this asset in a more planned and disciplined way.

As personalized communication and service become more important to affluent clients, the effect of too much inventory (too many small clients) is even worse for those in the service industry. In today's world of financial advice, too much inventory means that affluent clients receive less personal communication and less service than they expect.

Everyone is aware that time is a precious commodity, but many advisors struggle in this area because they don't manage their priorities properly. Freeing time to strengthen relationships with top clients should be a *top priority*. It *is* for Elite Advisors. Freeing time for relationship-marketing activities should also be a priority.

Having too many smaller clients interferes with priority management, which generates too much reactive activity and too much stress. The bottom line: if you have too many clients, you can't be an Elite Advisor serving an affluent clientele. This is a bandwidth issue that's at the heart of effective practice management.

Elite Advisors take bandwidth and inventory seriously. They conduct a yearly analysis of their client base. Staying lean helps them proactively service clients, proactively market their practice, and proactively maintain their sanity. This yearly ritual often includes delegating smaller, less complex clients to other advisors, a call center, etc.

Is this process scary? For many advisors, yes, especially the first couple of times that smaller clients are jettisoned. But Elite Advisors know that giving away clients is the right thing to do—for the clients and the advisor. They know that handing off smaller clients translates into more time servicing top clients and more time devoted to finding new clients.

Recommended Total Households

We're often asked to recommend the total number of households an advisor should handle. How many is *too* many? It depends on the advisor, the profile of the clients, the service model and the firm's infrastructure. Sticking with the product/service comparison, think about your "turnover." How many clients can you properly service in one year?

We use a tool with our coaching clients that can help determine turnover based on the level of service provided to each segment of clients. The objective is to analyze your book of business, determine how many clients you can properly service, and make the necessary adjustments. Keeping it simple for the purposes of this book, we suggest you analyze the following:

Bandwidth Calculator

- What service model do you have in place for each tier of clients?
- How many hours are required for each element in the service model?
- How many times will each service element be performed per client, per year?
- Who is involved in performing the services?
- How many hours of client service have you planned for the year?
- How many hours of client service does this equal per week?
- Are there enough hours available in the week?

There are three options for advisors who discover that they don't have enough hours in the week to provide the desired level of service:

1. Scale back service (not a good idea for affluent clients).
2. Scale back the client base (good idea for smaller clients).
3. Hire another advisor or relationship manager (good idea—*if* you have more profitable clients than you can service; bad idea if you have too many non-profitable clients).

If this were a business school case study, the answer would be clear: make transitional arrangements for non-profitable clients, focus energy on the larger clients, and only hire when you have more profitable clients than you can service.

Client Segmentation and Service Models

Over the past ten years, most advisors have done a fairly good job of segmenting their client bases. Many have even learned how to give away smaller clients. However, more needs to be done. The idea is simple: priority attention must be given to clients generating the most revenue and this attention must be highly professional as well as personal. Easier said than done, we know.

First, take a clinical view of your households, determining which generate most of your annual revenue. Let's say you have 250 households (down from 500hhs a few years ago), and you want to determine which clients are responsible for the most revenue. You'll never stray too far from the 80/20 principle, whether it's 20 percent of your client base or 20 households.

The days of attempting to be all things to all clients are long gone. Our research tells us that Elite Teams and Elite Advisors have two service models: one for top clients generating approximately 80 percent of revenue, and a scaled back model for the remaining (but still profitable) clients.

To improve your service model, you must also determine who will serve as the primary relationship manager for each client and the tasks associated with that role. As advisors move toward smaller client bases, they need to move away from the A, B, C and D segmentation, embracing the principle of two service models for a limited inventory of clients.

The following service models are based on our research on Elite Teams. Because there is little difference between an advisor and a team when it comes to service models, we thought the following differentiation between platinum and gold service models would be useful:

Service Elements	Platinum	Gold
• 24/7 Cell phone access	Yes	No
• Face-to-Face Reviews	2/year	1/year
• Telephone Reviews	2/year	1/year
• Intimate Client Event Invitations	4/year	Selective
• Telephone contact with a team member	Weekly	As needed
• Surprise and delight	2/year	Selective
• Dinner with the Team Leader	3/year	None
• Birthday event	1–2/year	None
• Birthday card	1–2/year	1–2/year
• Max time for returned phone calls	2 hours	24 hours

It is important to consider every service element above for *both* husband and wife. We've seen advisors create problems by hosting a birthday dinner for one spouse while neglecting the other. To get around this, we've seen some creative advisors recognize half birthdays—a celebration halfway between the couple's birthdays. They get one half of the cake in one variety and the other half in another variety. Half birthdays aside, what's done for one spouse, from a personalized service perspective, should be counter-balanced with something for the other.

The challenge many teams encounter with this personalized, high-level, dual-spouse service is that they offer too many levels of service: A-client service, B-client service, C-client service, D-client service, etc., which creates tremendous internal confusion and inefficiencies. We also see teams providing the "one-size-fits-all" standard, which results in no real standard at all. Even with the best of intentions, things always fall through the cracks, and top clients rarely get the level of attention they deserve.

The following is an example of how this analysis opened the eyes of a top advisor when it came to prioritizing time, service models, roles and responsibilities.

George's client base had been trimmed to 205 households, of which he considered 110 to be good and profitable clients. They generated approximately 88 percent of his production. George hadn't created a service model for the 95 smaller households still on the books, since he was planning to give them to a junior advisor. At issue was the time allocated versus the net revenue generated per household.

After a few calculations, George determined that his top 25 clients, his most profitable households, averaged $2.5 million in assets per household, generating about $25,000 per household annually. The remaining eighty-five households averaged $500,000 in assets, generating $5,000 per household annually. George had developed what he considered a high-touch service model, which he'd used for the past two years.

George's Service Model:

In-person reviews—4 per year.

Outreach communications—6 per year.

Immediate response to all incoming requests.

Client education events (small groups)—4 per year.

Social lunch or dinner with spouses—1-3 per year.

Intimate Client Events—3 per year.

The above service model was used for each of his 110 clients, which had him servicing clients paying $5,000 per year the same as clients paying $25,000 per year. Upon closer examination George realized that he'd really been using two service models, since he was socializing with his top 25 clients but not the others. The following exercise opened George's eyes. George looked at time-value of his services with his top 25 in one category (without the socializing) and the remaining 85 households in the other category.

Top 25 Clients—Platinum

- *Assets - $62,500,000.*
- *Gross (1 percent fee)—$625,000.*
- *Net Revenue (45 percent payout)—$281,250 ($11,250 per household).*
- *Quarterly review—1.5 hours each, 6 hours per year.*
- *Review Preparation—2 hours each, 8 hours per year.*
- *Outreach communication—1 hour per year.*
- *Handling issues—1 hour per year.*

Service Time—16 hours per client annually

****Hourly Rate—$703 generated per hour spent servicing each client*

85 Remaining Clients—Gold

- *Assets - $42,500,000.*
- *Gross (1 percent fee)—$425,000.*
- *Net Revenue (45 percent payout)—$191,250 ($2,250 per household).*
- *Quarterly review—1.5 hours each, 6 hours per year.*
- *Review Preparation—2 hours each, 8 hours per year.*
- *Out-reach communication—1 hour per year.*
- *Handling issues—1 hour per year.*
- *Service Time—16 hours per client annually*

****Hourly Rate—$141 generated per hour spent servicing each client*

At this stage, George didn't want to quantify the "time-value" of socializing with his top clients, because it often included his relationship marketing.

Addressing his basic service model, however, was another issue. He determined that only his top 25 clients required face-to-face quarterly reviews, with the remaining 85 households receiving three 45-minute conference call reviews and just one in-person review per year. His goal was to hand-off the relationship management of these clients to his junior advisor within 18 months. Meanwhile, because he still managed these relationships, this would save him 2 hours per client, per year.

Next, he determined that he was spending far too much time preparing for each review, top 25 and 85 alike. In this case, he decided to expand the responsibilities of the junior advisor, and part of his grooming would include updating and organizing the files for upcoming reviews. With these 85 clients, George figured that the junior advisor would need 15 minutes to peruse the files. For the top 25 households, George figured he'd need 30 minutes. He also figured that if he tightened-up the meetings with a written agenda, they would only take an hour instead of 90 minutes.

Granted, none of these projections are the definitive time-value figures (he didn't calculate his junior advisor's time or spreading four hours of educational events over the clients who attended), but they served a purpose. George was able to prioritize his time and begin to get a handle on the time-value of each client.

It's easy to understand why so many advisors avoid this exercise. It's tedious work. It forces you to make calculated assumptions, as well as to analyze the current status of your time, which typically leads to making changes. In George's case, he needed to tighten his service model and elevate his junior advisor to relationship manager of 85 healthy and profitable households. He was uncomfortable letting go of personally managing those 85 relationships, but after he compared their time-value status with that of his top 25 clients, he *knew* what he had to do.

Working with Support Personnel

Roles and Responsibilities: The State of the Relationship

Let's face it: support personnel have always presented a conundrum for advisors. Changing the titles from sales assistant to more professional varietals such as client associate, client service associate, etc., rings hollow without corresponding structural changes.

The dirty little industry secret is that few if any marketing promises can be delivered without the help of first-class support personnel committed to delivering Ritz Carlton service with FedEx efficiency. We consider this level of support *indispensable* for advisors who are serious about achieving long-term success.

The relationship between Elite Advisors and support personnel can be best described as a partnership. They must work well together, achieve clarity regarding roles and responsibilities, have open lines of communication, and be on the same page when it comes to relationship management and relationship marketing. Elite Advisors have mastered the art of delegation and empowerment, and their support personnel are consistently up to the challenge.

The natural sequence for determining (or refining) roles and responsibilities is after the client base has been segmented into two tiers (platinum and gold) and the service models have been created. Once these are completed, you're ready to conduct a time-value assessment for each tier, which will help determine which responsibilities and/or tasks to get off your plate.

The financial crisis has placed a spotlight on affluent client retention and the role personalized service plays in strengthening loyalty. Affluent investors aren't fully blaming their financial advisors for investment performance, but they *are* holding those advisors accountable for the quality of service they've been receiving. Excellent support personnel are essential to providing quality service and enhancing quality communication between the firm and the client.

In an effort to help advisors address this challenge, the Oechsli Institute conducted a study on financial advisors and support personnel.[8] Our objective was to develop a roadmap to the ideal advisor/assistant relationship.

The following graph shows key areas of importance to advisors with regards to their primary assistant. It also shows the advisors' performance rankings of assistants in each criteria. As you will see, there are significant gaps in each area. The following 18 criteria were rated most important in a primary assistant:

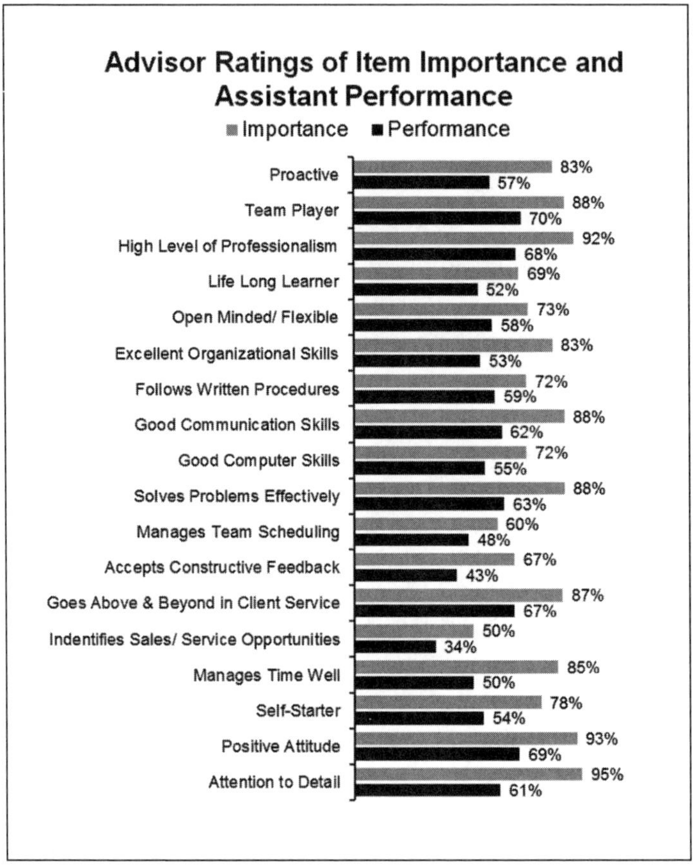

Oechsli Institute Administrative Assistant Research

Oechsli Institute Administrative Assistant Research

Taking a closer look at these gaps raises a series of questions: Is there clarity in roles and responsibilities? Do assistants know what's expected? Are they being properly trained to perform their roles? Is communication between advisors and assistants clear and ongoing? Are the assistants being monitored and reviewed properly?

For many advisors, the quick answer to many of these questions is, "no," which raises another two questions: "Is the right person in the role?" and "Do I have enough support?"

Fifty-seven percent of financial advisors share an assistant or don't have access to support, so it's important for advisors and management to address this issue for what it is—a serious handicap in servicing the affluent. Sorry advisors, we don't recommend that firms increase their expenses by providing every advisor with a personal assistant. Why? Our research tells us that only a minority of advisors would capitalize on the additional support.

The secret to growing your business, regardless of your level of support, is treating your support personnel as "team members." We apply the word *team* not just to advisors or multiple support staff. Your team can consist of your assistant (even if shared), your internal specialists, your external partners (CPAs, attorneys, etc.) and anyone else who contributes to your client service or marketing efforts.

Factors Impacting Assistant Performance

Compatibility between advisor and personal assistant is essential. Although this seems like another piece of common sense, the gaps in perceived job performance revealed by our study indicate that it's a big issue. Not surprisingly, assistants rate their overall performance higher than advisors rate their performance. (Assistants are also more likely to rate themselves as "underpaid.")

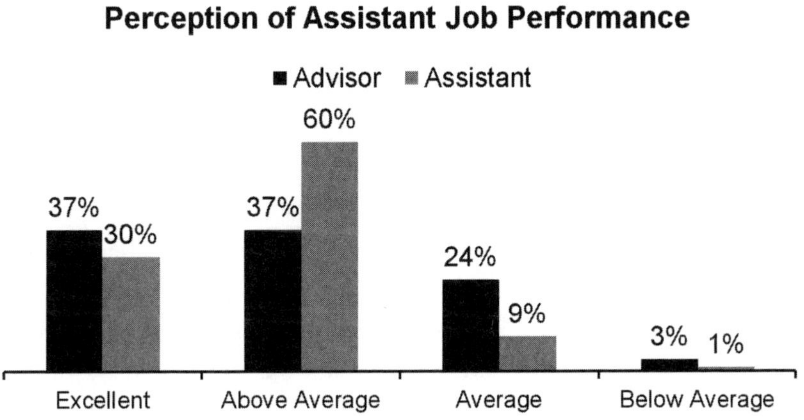

Oechsli Institute Administrative Assistant Research

No single thing will immediately impact an assistant's overall performance. But there are a number of contributing factors that we were able to identify:

Length of Service. It seems natural that the longer an assistant works with an advisor, the better the overall working relationship and performance. The fact that assistants who have worked with an advisor less than one year rated higher in the "excellent" categories than those with even three or five years' experience suggests that a "honeymoon" period is likely involved. In short, it takes about a year for advisors to accurately gauge the overall performance of an assistant.

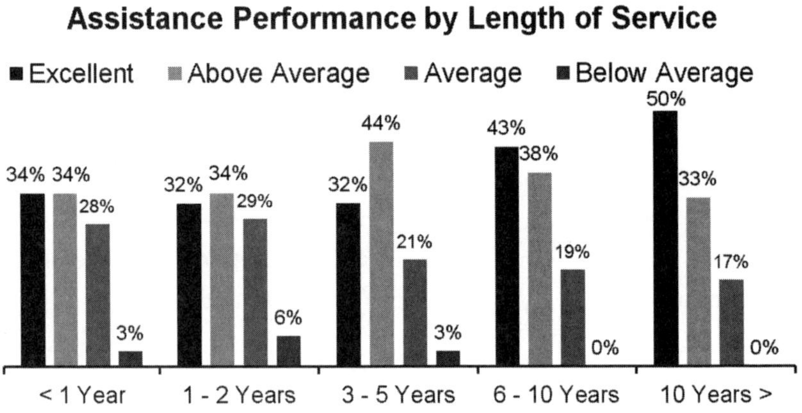

Oechsli Institute Administrative Assistant Research

Training. The training of assistants is all over the board. It should come as no surprise that assistants who were personally mentored received the best performance evaluations, followed by those who had received firm-based training. Our definition of "ad-hoc" training is simple: no real training. This is why it rated lowest in terms of job performance. Because of the personal nature of the advisory business, we recommend that assistants receive a blend of mentoring and firm-based training, and that advisors be actively involved.

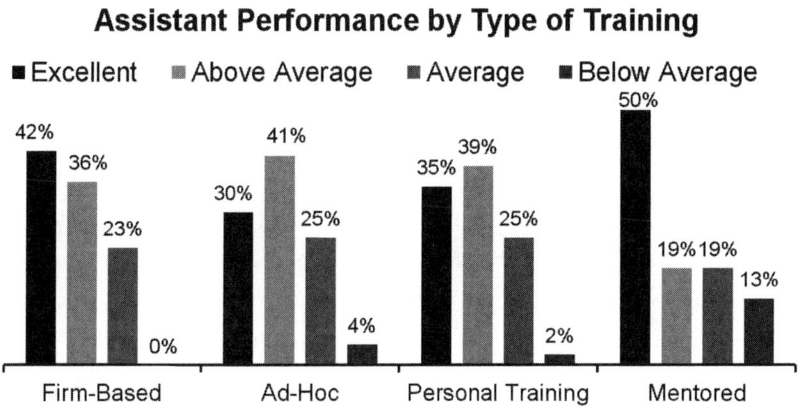

Oechsli Institute Administrative Assistant Research

Communication. Healthy communication means more than engaging in reactive dialogue throughout the day. The best advisor/assistant relationships are based on sharing business goals, defining the role, establishing performance expectations, aligning compensation to business goals and performance, instilling accountability and conducting structured weekly meetings.

As you can see in the following chart, advisors and assistants don't agree on even the frequency of their communication, much less the effectiveness. In other words, healthy communication is common sense, but not always common practice.

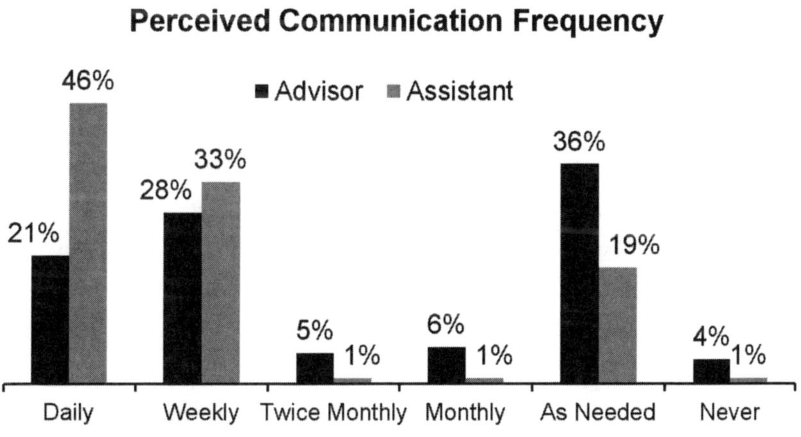

Oechsli Institute Administrative Assistant Research

Advisor/Assistant Action Plan

Elite Advisors recognize the importance of support personnel, and are willing to invest time, energy and resources into developing excellence within this role. It's no coincidence that they reap numerous rewards from these efforts, including loyal support personnel, loyal affluent clients, positive word-of-mouth and an energized working environment—to name a few. Elite Advisors understand that for them to attain and retain elite status, they need indispensable support personnel. Every financial advisor should be working toward this objective.

The following is a brief action plan to help you continually improve your relationships with support personnel:

1. **Discuss your assistant's performance regarding the 18 Criteria.** This should be part of an overall discussion about team performance. What could be done better? Ask your assistant(s) to self-score on each criterion with 1 being poor and 10 being excellent. Then conduct your own analysis and meet with your assistant(s) to compare results. This exercise should identify two or three things that you, as a team, could be doing better. Many performance gaps involve the advisor as much as the assistant.
2. **Conduct weekly team meetings.** Meet with your assistant(s) every week at the same time and day of the week. This is a structured, short meeting with a preset agenda. It's a great way to keep track of the little things that would otherwise be forgotten (project updates, small gifts to clients, client service issues, etc.). See next section on team meetings for more details.
3. **Discuss your quirks.** We all have differences in how we like to communicate, structure our day, handle clients, and so on. If you want top clients to get better turnaround times than other clients, you must communicate this desire to your assistant(s). Anything less than clear communication—including specific action steps—will cause one or both of you to become frustrated.
4. **Celebrate your successes as a team.** Whenever you bring in a new client—or a current client voices satisfaction with your

work—celebrate as a team. It's easy to dwell on what isn't working, missing opportunities for positive reinforcement. Celebration might come in the form of a drink after work or a small gift when the assistant has gone the extra mile for a client. Even a verbal "thank you" helps. The little things matter.

We understand that your assistant is probably being pulled in several different directions and that you're not the only one vying for his or her attention. At the end of the day, it's all about relationship management. If you spend a little more time with your assistant, you'll get a little more in return. Take a few minutes to discuss the challenges your assistant may be having with a project, ask him/her if she wants lunch when you're going out, ask how his/her day is going, and so on. One of the biggest differences between elite teams and the rest is communication between advisors and assistants.

Effective Team Meetings

We got a call a while back from a junior member of a team we were coaching. He said, "I know you're recommending that we revive our team meetings. Let me tell you why we're resisting." The junior member goes on to tell us how "painful" these team meetings had been. They involved the senior advisor on the team hashing and re-hashing sales targets, talking about how things were done "back when I got started," and so on. After about 45 minutes of this, everyone was exhausted and the meeting adjourned. Before long, team members were coming up with excuses for why they had to miss the meeting. Can you blame them? This is why many advisors see team meetings as a waste of time. They've been part of, even possibly led, ineffective team meetings.

Most Elite Advisors meet with their teams on a weekly basis, while only 47% of the general population of teams can say the same.[9] Believe it or not, most elite team members actually look forward to these meetings. They are well-structured, held at the same time and place and each team member knows what he or she is responsible for reporting.

We are going to walk you through three important areas with regards to running effective team meetings. These apply whether you're on a mega team with twenty members or if it's just you and a shared assistant:

- Scheduling and Preparation
- Agenda
- Ground Rules

Scheduling and Preparation

Team meetings should be scheduled at the same time on the same day of every week. Many teams find it helpful to have their meeting on Monday mornings to "frame" the rest of the week. Regardless of the time you select, consistency is the key. This eliminates the "I have a client meeting to go to" or "I wasn't sure if we were meeting or not." The team meeting *is happening*, and nobody should have anything else scheduled during that time.

The team leader may or may not be the person who should schedule and lead the meetings. We've often seen this task delegated, with superior results. A key support person with organizational skills and knowledge of the inner workings of the practice will usually host a better meeting than a busy team leader, who might be great at relationship management but not so great at meeting planning. This is the essence of "letting go and gaining control."

Each team member should have responsibilities for the team meeting, and these should be spelled out in writing before your next meeting. For example, the team leader might be responsible for the pipeline report; an assistant might be responsible for upcoming meeting planning and client event updates, and so on. This avoids "if I remember correctly, I think we're . . ." scenarios. Each team member should provide a detailed reporting on his/her assigned topic.

Agenda

Elite teams have meetings with written agendas. Some of the agenda items will be standard (included each week), while others will be determined by the tasks at hand. Although it might seem redundant to include the same agenda items every week, forcing a discussion around these topics makes certain they're addressed. For instance, we all understand that handwritten thank you notes are important, but we often forget to write them. If one of your standard agenda items is "Thank you notes from last week," you're much less likely to forget.

The following is a sample meeting agenda that works well:

Team Meeting Agenda

- Welcome
- Last week recap
- Meetings this week
  - What preparation is needed?
  - What do we know about this person on a personal level?
  - What is our strategic intent?
- Opportunities to get social with clients this week (lunches, events, etc.)
- Update on key prospects
- Client event updates
- Surprise and delight intelligence uncovered
- Names sourced
- Handwritten thank you notes from last week
- Any vacation days over next two weeks
- Important updates from the firm/external vendors
- Other projects

This type of agenda also helps to keep the meeting on task. Meetings should last no longer than an hour, with the agenda as a visual representation of all topics to be discussed. If you linger on one item too long, it's time to pick up the pace.

Team Meeting Ground Rules

Every meeting needs ground rules. Many teams don't meet because of members' bad experiences with team meetings in the past—e.g., certain individuals talked the whole time, there were scheduling problems, nothing was accomplished, etc. All of these issues can be avoided with the right leadership and ground rules:

1. *Meetings are Held Regardless of Who's Out.* Team meetings are held even if one or more team members are absent (including the team leader). All it takes is one or two missed meetings to derail the whole process.
2. *Attendees Must Take Turns.* Meetings are not to become a soapbox for any one person, especially the team leader. It's the job of the meeting facilitator to keep meetings moving forward.
3. *Meetings Will Start and End on Time.* Do not wait for stragglers to show up, or extend a meeting beyond its allotted time without the permission of the attendees.
4. *Attendees Must Come Prepared.* Each team member should come prepared to discuss their assigned topic, or prepared to be called out. If you're meeting on Monday morning, encourage the team to prepare on the Friday afternoon before they leave for the weekend. Rushing around on Monday morning is no way to start the week.
5. *Attendees Must Commit to Specific Action Items.* Meetings will be conducted in the spirit of "Who will do what by when?" Action items must have a clear "owner" and clear deadlines.

Five Common Practice Management Mistakes

We thought it would be fun to borrow a page from Charlie Munger's decision-making process and invert practice management (for more on Charlie Munger and inversion, read his 1986 Harvard commencement address). The following are 5 common practice management mistakes:

1. **Not linking practice management to servicing existing clients, strengthening client loyalty, and acquiring more clients.** In essence, practice management must be linked to your business plan. Granted, this assumes that you have a written business plan. If not, get busy. If you have a business plan, make sure

your practice management processes have a direct impact on your marketing efforts. For example, segmenting clients and creating service models increases top client contact and top client word-of-mouth influence. Holding effective team meetings increases the odds that you'll surprise and delight affluent clients—deepening their loyalty.

2. **Getting lost in process overload.** Often, this is symptomatic of a failure to link practice management to the business plan. When policies and procedures take on a life of their own (excessive paperwork, duplicate procedures, redundancies, etc.), two questions need to be answered: A) is this procedure necessary for delivering the promised services in an efficient and effective manner; and B) is this procedure interfering with growth?
3. **Developing avoidance patterns.** People are creatures of habit. We tend to gravitate toward activities that lie within our comfort zones. Herein lays the irony: very few advisors enjoy the operational aspects of their businesses. Most enjoy the adrenaline rush that comes with acquiring a new affluent client. Yet, as distasteful as paperwork might seem, most advisors don't have to go outside their comfort zones to handle operational issues, whereas rainmaking activities often force them outside of their comfort zones. Consequently, advisors who get involved with tasks that should be delegated unwittingly develop avoidance patterns—a bad habit. Practice management activities should never interfere with a financial advisor's marketing activities!
4. **Lack of leadership.** Elite financial advisors are leaders. They take a leadership role within their practices, with their clients, COIs, referral alliance partners and prospects. This requires a vision for the practice, taking inventory, defining areas of responsibility, delegating properly, communicating clearly, and consistently inspecting what's expected. In other words, leadership is hands-on work.
5. **Failing to prioritize procedures.** Not every practice management task is created equal. A worthwhile exercise is to create an outline of each task that must be done on a regular basis. These are often divided according to the major components of your

practice (business development, operational efficiency, wealth management and client loyalty). Discuss these procedures as a team and gather consensus on priorities.

This chapter was built to help you with some of the basics of practice management—having the right service models, working in-sync with your assistant, hosting effective team meetings, and so on. This is all about running your business like a business. You can only get so far with great sales or investment skills. Your business will never reach its full potential without the right operations.

Remember, practice management is a work in progress, even for Elite Advisors. Every time your practice changes by introducing a new service, adding a new team member, or any other significant happening, you must revisit your policies, procedures, and make sure everyone is on the same page. Are roles and responsibilities still clear? Should we eliminate a certain procedure? These are some of the many questions that must be asked.

Key Takeaways:

- Many advisors have too many service models (A,B,C,D) which creates internal confusion. We suggest creating two service models—one for your top affluent clients and one for everyone else.
- Make sure your service models include personal touches for your top affluent clients (lunches, dinners, surprise and delight) and include both spouses.
- Team meetings are the glue that holds the team together, even if it's just you and a shared assistant. They help you stay on track with important initiatives.
- Team meetings should be held every week at the same time and be built from a standard agenda.
- Your assistant is part of your brand. Hands-on training and daily communication helps make certain you're working in tandem.
- Many advisors have too many clients, which stifles their growth. Calculate your bandwidth and determine how many clients you can properly service, while maintaining your marketing efforts for ideal clients.

6

Wealth Management

> *Factoid: 40% of those with $1mm or more in investable assets say their advisor is doing an excellent job of financial planning.*[1]

We've all heard the refrain, "I've seen it before—the markets go down and everyone screams about change. Then the markets recover and everything goes back to business as usual."

Not with the Great Recession.

We often use the following quote from the *Harvard Business Review,* but it bears repeating:

> "In times of crisis, people's behaviors and perspective change irrevocably. As we begin to emerge from a worldwide economic collapse, it will be critical that business leaders understand what the new norms are—and most important—how to adapt."[10]

Adapting means change. This goes beyond the gender shift. Our current research is clear regarding what today's affluent investor is looking for from a financial advisor—comprehensive wealth management with a strong emphasis on protecting that wealth.

The days of placing singular focus on buying and selling securities is over. For many advisors, it's time for a change—change that goes beyond *claiming* to provide comprehensive wealth management solutions because you have the ability to provide such services, while primarily focusing on assets under management. We're talking about actually *providing* wealth management services in a structured manner.

Today's affluent investor wants an advisor who is able to oversee every aspect of the family's financial affairs—a solutions provider for the multi-dimensional aspects of the family finances. Investors don't want a one-dimensional advisor, whether it's an investment advisor or someone specializing in insurance solutions. They want someone who can coordinate it all—to serve as the family physician of finances. Elite Advisors understand this, and have already adjusted their deliverables accordingly.

Most financial advisors now conduct personal reviews with their clients. Some conduct these reviews quarterly; others on an annual basis. How an advisor conducts the reviews is very telling. What we've discovered is that a review isn't always a review. The following are two actual cases of reviews with an affluent client. We're providing only a snapshot of these review meetings, but you should be able to gain an understanding of the structure these advisors apply.

Example 1 (Ron):

Most of Ron's client review meetings center around performance. The client comes to his office (usually just the male of the household, since according to Ron, most of the wives don't want to be involved) and a few pleasantries are exchanged. They jump right into the client's investment performance, positions and returns. The client departs, another few months go by, and they're called back for another review. Ron typically dominates the meeting, either defending his investment selections in excruciating detail (if they've fallen short of expectations) or subtly patting himself on the back by explaining how he made his investment decisions if they met or exceeded expectations.

In both scenarios, the client might ask a few questions, which Ron will answer in his typical manner—in great detail. By the time the meeting concludes and the client departs, the 80/20 listening-to-speaking ratio has been obliterated.

There are few discussions about financial planning, insurance protection or estate planning, and when they *do* occur, they're usually initiated by the client. As a result, Ron gains very little insight as to what's happening in the client's family; what their children are doing, what worries them, what they're excited about, etc. Without an ongoing stream of intelligence, Ron has limited himself to talking only about what he knows.

Although Ron may claim that he's handling every aspect of his clients' financial affairs, his reviews tell a different story. It's no wonder that Ron finally admitted to us that he sometimes has trouble getting clients to come in for reviews.

Example 2 (Susan):
Susan's affluent clients actually look forward to her review meetings. They are thoroughly educated about the structure of their client/advisor relationship. It begins when they're still prospects. Susan explains how she communicates with clients, her review process, and when each aspect of the client's financial life will be discussed. Before they become clients, they understand that the reviews are *their reviews*, and that it's important for both husband and wife to attend. Part of Susan's client acquisition process is a *Communication Agreement* personalized for every client, and signed by Susan and the new clients. It outlines the rules of engagement; who will contact whom and how often this contact will occur.

All of this provides the context within which Susan manages each affluent client relationship. Providing this type of structure makes her value more tangible. It's also a key part of her client-acquisition efforts, as prospective clients rarely have this type of structure with their soon-to-be former advisor.

Each affluent client gets three personal meetings throughout the year, with a pre-set agenda. Each meeting is distinct, with one focused on asset allocation/performance/fees, one focused on financial planning, and one focused on protection (more on this system of "themed reviews" later in the chapter).

This structure helps Susan cover every angle of her clients' finances—from budgeting and cash flow, to philanthropy, to having the right outside experts. She has a *system* for addressing each issue with both spouses.

Even though each meeting has a different theme, complete with a pre-set agenda, they all have a common thread. Susan begins every review by reminding her clients that this is *their meeting*, and by asking each spouse this personal question: "Is there anything that's been on your mind that you'd like to discuss?" According to Susan, it's common for this question to prompt conversations that cover the key points she wanted to discuss on her pre-set agenda.

As you might guess, Susan's clients find this type of personal, professional service worthy of sharing with friends, family and colleagues. This is yet another example of service linked to marketing.

Given the intangible nature of wealth management, we've found that a handful of simple questions can serve as a helpful exercise. Ask everyone on your team to independently think about, and then write out, their answers to these questions:

- How would you define comprehensive wealth management?
- What services are you currently providing to affluent clients?
- What is your system for ensuring that each affluent client receives these services?
- Can you articulate your wealth management process to affluent clients *and* prospects?

After answering these questions yourself, establish a day and time to meet with the team to discuss their answers. Your objective is to get team members involved, discover what they're actually thinking, lead a group discussion and get everyone on the same page.

This is the type of exercise that's easy for advisors to blow-off by assuming everyone is on the same page. Do *not* make this assumption! Elite Advisors never take their wealth management process for granted. Instead, approach this task with two questions: "What did I discover?" and "Is there a need to add more service offerings?"

Services the Affluent Want

Regardless of whether a particular wealth management solution is profitable, time consuming or enjoyable, Elite Advisors deliver what affluent clients need and want. We've said it many times, but our research on today's affluent is clear; they want a solutions provider to oversee the multi-dimensional aspect of their family's financial affairs. This is precisely the role that Elite Advisors play.

As we list the full complement of wealth management services, remember the following: although these are areas in which affluent investors want advice and guidance, the process is very fluid. We're living in a globalized and digitized world—one where change has become the norm. With that caveat, think in terms of whether you have the expertise within your team or practice to deliver all of these services. If you don't, that's okay, but you're going to need to coordinate with appropriate outside experts.

Obviously, not every affluent client will need or want all of these services. Your responsibility is to have a working knowledge of each, know when to introduce them, and know how to access the necessary expertise.

9 Key Wealth Management Areas

The following are 9 Key Wealth Management Areas pulled straight from our research on the affluent; these are services that affluent clients want. You may be offering some or all of these, but as you read through each service, make note of your current involvement in each area and determine any necessary action steps.

1) Banking Services
Current Involvement: ________________________________
Actions Steps Needed: ________________________________

2) Insurance Planning
Current Involvement: ________________________________
Actions Steps Needed: ________________________________

3) Asset Management
Current Involvement: ______________________________
Actions Steps Needed: ______________________________

4) Cash Flow Management
Current Involvement: ______________________________
Actions Steps Needed: ______________________________

5) Education Planning
Current Involvement: ______________________________
Actions Steps Needed: ______________________________

6) Tax Planning
Current Involvement: ______________________________
Actions Steps Needed: ______________________________

7) Retirement Planning
Current Involvement: ______________________________
Actions Steps Needed: ______________________________

8) Estate Planning
Current Involvement: ______________________________
Actions Steps Needed: ______________________________

9) Charitable Giving
Current Involvement: ______________________________
Actions Steps Needed: ______________________________

Themed Review Meetings

Imagine visiting your primary care physician on a regular basis for the same checkup—blood pressure, height/weight and cholesterol. Year after year, your annual physical covers the same three items. Chances are that you wouldn't be excited about your visits and you'd start to wonder about your physician's concern of your overall health. What's more, it's unlikely that you'd speak highly about your physician when talking to friends and family.

Stick with us on this loose analogy. We realize that most physicians are not really overseeing the multidimensional aspects of their patient's medical health, but if we focus on Concierge Medicine, where doctors charge a retainer and focus on fewer families, the similarities are numerous and meaningful.

> "[Patients using Concierge Medicine] have longer visits, around-the-clock access to one of five physicians, comprehensive wellness and prevention screenings and on-time office appointments within 24 hours of a request. This new model allowed doctors to offer more personalized care that in turn increased patient and professional satisfaction."[11]

Put yourself in an affluent client's shoes. Wouldn't you want a concierge advisor? High level service . . . a comprehensive plan...what's not to like? Nearly every advisor has the ability and resources to provide high level service and a broad range of services. Most simply lack the structure or initiative to do it consistently.

Instead of having clients attend meeting after meeting with the same agenda (or no agenda), we suggest having three to four themed reviews throughout the year, with an agenda that specifies when each area of their financial life will be addressed.

We recognize that every financial advisor has different areas of expertise and different processes for working with clients. That's OK. The secret is fitting your service elements into a clear structure that both clients and prospects can understand.

Creating themed reviews benefits you on two fronts:

- *Positioning.* Clients are more aware of what you're doing for them. In effect, you remind them of the value you're delivering. Affluent prospects will also see a concrete example (tangible evidence) of your comprehensive wealth management services.
- *Structure.* You ensure that every affluent client is given a full

array of ancillary services—scheduled meetings with outside experts, reviews of old insurance policies, meetings with the children, etc.

Done properly, these reviews should be command performances that are naturally woven into your marketing/branding, as well as the professional services you're delivering to affluent clients.

Your first step is to analyze everything you are currently doing for top clients. Next, determine what you *could* be doing for them. The third step is to decide *when* each element is analyzed/reviewed with the client. All of this culminates in a written outline that can be given to each affluent client and prospect. The following is a brief outline of the structure you could provide to a series of three client reviews throughout the year. Your actual agenda would be more detailed based on your specific wealth management process.

Example:

Review 1—Portfolio Review

- Asset Allocation
- Performance
- Fee Discussion—Making client fully aware of fees being paid

Review 2—Financial Planning

- Financial Plan Update
- Net Worth Statement Update
- Changes to your financial life (inheritance, marriage, etc.)
- Family discussion (kids and/or parents)

Review 3—Risk Audit

- What-if Scenarios
  —Wills
  —Estate Planning
  —Insurance (life, health, disability, long-term care, etc.)
- Outside Experts
  —Current professionals used
  —Ratings for each professional (1–5)

*Consider having the same meeting in the same quarter of the year—i.e., Q2 is always about Financial Planning. This creates structure, and helps your staff prepare more efficiently.

Once again, this is all about creating a *process* for working with today's affluent. If you're introducing services "as needed," you're probably missing some key opportunities to help your clients.

Going to themed reviews is just one of many ways to strengthen your client review process. The following are 5 Tips for Effective Affluent Client Reviews. We've pulled these from our coaches who've helped thousands of advisors with their client review process.

5 Tips for Effective Affluent Client Reviews:

1. *Prepare for relationship building.* Reviewing client notes, gathering intelligence online, and thinking about the client's friends, family and hobbies prior to the meeting, helps you prepare a thoughtful list of questions and conversation topics. Always begin every review like Susan, asking each spouse if there is anything they'd like to discuss.
2. *Conduct some reviews outside the office.* Going to the homes of affluent clients for selective reviews helps to get the spouses involved and opens the dialogue about their family and personal lives. It also helps you strengthen the personal side of your relationships by getting a better understanding of their families. You're seeing their photos on the walls, taking note of the books on their coffee tables and getting to know them in a relaxed environment.
3. *Engage both spouses in the review process.* Finance is a family discussion. Even if one family member doesn't want to be involved in every decision, he or she should still be engaged at the appropriate times. If nothing else, involve this person in the financial planning and goals conversation. It's important to remember that affluent women have more influence in their family's financial affairs and higher expectations from financial advisors.

Don't just involve both spouses: take time to *understand* both spouses.

4. *Create a short overview of your review process.* Share it with clients during the review (as a reminder of what is occurring) *and* with affluent prospects. This is another way to demonstrate your value—to *showcase* your comprehensive wealth management services and give clients/prospects something to talk about in their spheres-of-influence.
5. *Link service with marketing.* Affluent client reviews are an excellent opportunity to source names from your clients' spheres-of-influence and to find information that might elicit a small surprise gift. Elite Advisors are able to uncover this information through the course of the natural conversation that occurs during the review. These little things, done consistently, are what contribute to Elite Advisors growing their business.

There's nothing overly complex about running an effective review meeting, but you'll limit your effectiveness if you're just "going through the motions" in your reviews. Just remember to listen effectively, engage the family, and put some structure around your process.

Engaging Both Spouses in Wealth Management

We've heard this often from advisors: "my clients' spouses don't want to be involved." Not so fast, my friend! True or not, you *need* both spouses involved. We've said it before but it's worth repeating. Clients make better decisions when both spouses are involved. Advisors develop deeper loyalty and have double the COI penetration. What's not to like?

In most of the cases where one spouse isn't involved, it's for one of the following reasons:

- The advisor hasn't made an effort to engage that spouse in the past.
- The advisor engaged the spouse in the past, but used too much

investment-speak at the meeting, so now the spouse doesn't want to come back.

- The advisor engaged the spouse in the past, but didn't give the spouse any attention during the meeting, so now the spouse doesn't want to come back.

Whatever the reason, advisors need to make a sincere effort to get non-participating spouses to participate. This is not as arduous as it may seem. Working with your team/assistant, audit your list of top clients. You want four dates beside each client household:

- Last business contact with spouse #1
- Last business contact with spouse #2
- Last social contact with spouse #1
- Last social contact with spouse #2

Working through this top client audit will likely reveal a few cases in which you need to re-engage the spouse. There are a number of ways to do this:

1. Call the non-participating spouse with two simple statements, "I know I spend most of the time talking with __________, but I wanted to catch up with you for a few minutes. Is there anything on your mind financially?"
2. Call the participating spouse to stress the importance of the non-participating spouse attending the next review meeting. Explain that it's critically important that you catch up with both of them regarding goals, protection and other important family issues.
3. Call either spouse and invite them as a couple to a lunch or dinner. Ask for the spouse's favorite restaurant. *That* is where you're going.

This simple exercise works. Think about it as a ninety-day effort to deepen client relationships. This might be two to three face-to-face contacts per week until you're up to date. After that, it's all about maintenance—making sure to engage both spouses, on a business and social level, indefinitely.

Key Takeaways:

- Wealth Management solutions are always changing. This chapter links directly to the chapter on Lifelong Learning as you're always updating your expertise.
- Being capable of providing a service and actually providing a service are two different things. What is your process for utilizing each service?
- Themed reviews are an excellent way to add structure to your process. Three reviews with three distinctly different agendas helps you provide a comprehensive approach.
- Print a copy of your client review agenda for use with prospects. It's tangible evidence of what you do.
- Engaging the spouses of your clients, depending on your proficiency with this in the past, can be hard work, but it's well worth the effort.
- Calling non-participating spouses and asking them, "Is there anything on your mind financially?" is a great way to begin the relationship building process.

7

Leadership

Factoid: During the financial crisis of 2008, only 13.8% increased the face time they spent with clients.[12]

Few topics are discussed with more reverence than leadership. Traditionally ascribed to monumental figures like George Washington, Abraham Lincoln and Winston Churchill (to name a few), leadership is rarely associated with everyday people—much less everyday people who are "just" doing their jobs.

However, the leadership spotlight often shines brightly on everyday people during challenging times. The decisions they make, the actions they take and the mental and physical strain become a part of future lore. Everyday leaders do their jobs—and *then* go beyond the call of duty. They elevate themselves above their peers who, for whatever reasons, are incapable of making decisions in tough times. Either that, or they make poor decisions or are paralyzed by the pressure. Whether it's a financial advisor calming panicked clients when the markets go bad or the firemen who enter burning buildings to save lives, leadership can be found every day . . . if we know what to look for.

Nothing illustrates this better than two very public incidents:

Cruise Liner Tragedy

You may recall hearing about the capsizing of the Italian luxury ship Costa Concordia, which caused thirty-two passengers to drown. On the night of January 13, 2012, the Costa Concordia hit a reef, sinking off the Mediterranean island of Isola del Giglio. The tragedy made headlines around the world.

It wasn't long before blame was being cast in many directions, but most media attention focused on Captain Francesco Schettino. Rumors started circulating immediately—"there was a twenty-five-year old dancer with the captain," "he was on the phone with a retired captain," "the close pass was a planned 'fly by' to salute a former captain on the island," and so on. We may never know exactly what happened, but Schettino became one of the most hated men in Italy overnight.

Two mistakes were well-documented. The first was perhaps the biggest: steering the ship within a few dozen meters of the coastline, grounding it, and sending guests into a panic.

His second blunder was far more memorable. When it became clear the cruise liner was sinking, Captain Schettino commandeered a lifeboat for himself and made a break for safety, leaving his passengers to fend for themselves. As reports began to surface, a sad reality became evident: the captain and his crew were among the first to jump ship.

The loss of life, the ensuing blame game, and the public outcry will not soon be forgotten. But as with most tragedies, there are leadership lessons to be learned.

Read through the following transcript of the conversation between Captain Francesco Schettino and Port Authority officials in Italy as the ship was going down.[13] It's a great example of leadership, or lack thereof, in action:

Port Authority: *Schettino, listen to me, there are people trapped onboard, now you go back, you will go with your rescue boat under the stern of the ship, there are some steps, you climb those steps and you get onboard and you get back to me letting me know how many people are on board. Is that clear to you? I am actually recording this conversation captain.*

[Inaudible, captain mumbles]

PA: *Speak in a loud voice.*

Captain: *So, the ship right now [inaudible]...*

PA: *Speak in a loud voice! Put your hand by the microphone to cover it and speak up! Is that clear?*

Captain: *So, right now the ship is tilted . . .*

PA: *I understand that. Listen to me, there are people that are getting off using the rope ladder on the stern side, you go back there and you go up that ladder the opposite way, you go onboard the ship and you tell me how many people [are there] and what they need. You tell me if there are children, women or people that need assistance and you give me a number for each one of these categories is that clear? Look Schettino, you may have saved yourself from the sea but (we'll) put you through a lot of trouble, it will be very bad for you! Get back on board for [expletive]'s sake!!!*

Captain: *Officer, please.*

PA: *There are no "pleases"! Get back on board! Please assure me that you are going back on board.*

Captain: *I am here on the rescue boat. I'm right here, I didn't go anywhere else, I'm here.*

PA: *What are you doing captain?*

Captain: *I'm here to coordinate rescue operations.*

PA: *What are you coordinating? Get back on board and coordinate rescue operations from onboard the ship.*

[silence, sound cuts out]

PA: *Get back on board! This is an order! You don't need to make any other assessment. You have declared that you have abandoned ship, therefore I'm in command. Get back on board right now is that clear?*

Captain: *I have spoken with the company, and there seem to be some people still onboard, possibly about one hundred.*

PA: *And you can't even give me a precise number? You say "there seem to be"?*

Captain: *Well, we were carrying out evacuation procedures, but now all the officers have gathered on the rescue boat with me.*

PA: *Why did you allow them to get off, Captain?*

Captain: *I didn't . . . We abandoned ship.*

PA: *And with 100 people still on board you abandon ship? [expletive]*

Captain: *I didn't abandon any ship... because the ship turned on its side quickly and we were catapulted into the water.*

PA: *We'll clarify later what actually happened... for now tell me everything that goes on, everything! Place yourself under the ship with your rescue boat and don't leave.*

Every time we re-read that transcript we find ourselves with a sickening feeling in the pit of our stomachs. Not only did this supposed leader, the captain of a major cruise liner, single-handedly create the crisis he faced by breaking maritime rules, he exhibited a complete disregard for anyone other than himself.

This calamity, much like the Great Recession, affected not only those directly involved, but friends, family and bystanders around the globe. This event has potential cruise passengers around the world re-thinking their vacations. What is the quality and reputation of the cruise liner? Who is the captain? What is the captain's history and competency? As we write, between this tragedy and other unfortunate cruise incidents, the major cruise lines are scrambling to fill their berths, offering serious discounts and other incentives to attempt to recover their customer base.

Would doing his job properly have prevented the accident? Of course, it would have.

Would effective leadership—doing his job under pressure—have minimized the scale of the tragedy? We will never know, but one would like to think so.

Today's affluent investors view the financial services industry in the same light as the surviving passengers of the Costa Concordia. They are asking questions that include:

Has my advisor prevented me from experiencing a financial disaster?
Is my advisor competent to guide me through challenging times?
Has my advisor spent time with me and my family to provide personal assurance about his advice?
Is my advisor really doing his job?
Is my advisor capable of doing his job?
What is the reputation of my advisor's firm?

In late-2008, just as the severity of the financial crisis was becoming known, only 13.8 percent of financial advisors were increasing the face time spent with their clients. Whether these advisors panicked at the collapse of the markets, didn't recognize the importance of these events, or just forgot to get around to it, 86.2 percent of financial advisors could have probably done more to calm their clients' concerns.

Of course, none of this is as tragic as abandoning passengers struggling in the Mediterranean while watching others drown, but nevertheless, it reveals poor leadership. Much like the 4,252 rescued passengers, these affluent clients are unlikely to forget that their advisors abandoned them in a time of need.

Elite Advisors did just the opposite. This is not to imply that Elite Advisors prevented affluent clients from being adversely affected by the crisis. Nearly every investor from Warren Buffett to Fred Wilpon and Saul Katz (owners of Sterling Equities and the New York Mets) felt the impact.

Unlike Captain Schettino, no financial advisor (not even Madoff) was responsible for the Great Recession. Our research tells us that the affluent are holding Wall Street and the United States government responsible—in that order. What financial advisors *are* being held accountable for is how they responded in the midst of the crisis.

This is where the actions of Elite Advisors further distanced them from all others. First, they worked feverishly to understand what was occurring—to figure out *what happened, what's likely to happen in the short term, and what actions should be taken.* Here's a snapshot of how Elite Advisors demonstrated leadership under pressure:

- They took a stand and crafted a simple but realistic storyline.
- They communicated the storyline to team members, support staff and junior advisors in order to assuage their fears and uncertainty. Elite Advisors understood the importance of getting their staff to communicate the storyline with confidence when panicky clients called.
- Elite Advisors took a proactive approach to contacting all clients

to calm their fears. The first contact was usually by phone; the second was a personal meeting with both the husband and wife.
- They increased their visibility in the community, addressing the issues and calming fears at a macro level.
- Elite Advisors increased their personal interaction with their professional referral alliance partners: CPAs, attorneys and the like.

All of this required time, attention to detail and hard work. Few if any of these advisors considered themselves leaders, but their execution under extreme pressure summoned their leadership qualities. These qualities never go unnoticed, so it's no coincidence that the "getting the job done" behaviors of Elite Advisors increased their appeal. They began attracting new affluent clients from within their own spheres-of-influence and those of their clients.

Mid-Flight Heroics

Let's examine "getting the job done" leadership as it applied to the "Miracle on the Hudson"—the January 15, 2009 flight piloted by Captain Chesley Sullenberger. Almost everyone has heard about the US Air flight from New York's LaGuardia airport to Charlotte, NC. The plane hit a large flock of birds shortly after take-off, disabling both engines.

Listening to the communications between Captain Sullenberger and the air traffic controllers, as they quickly and matter-of-factly outlined options for an emergency landing, is a textbook example of leadership under immense pressure. Their efforts were swift and coordinated. With very few alternatives, Sullenberger made a leadership decision to land the plane on the Hudson River. There were no guarantees of a safe landing (he'd never landed a jetliner in a river before), but he made the decision and acted. All of the passengers and crew members survived.

The following is a transcript of the communications between Sullenberger and an air traffic controller[14]:

Sullenberger: *Flaps up.*
Sullenberger: *After takeoff checklist complete.*

Sullenberger: *Birds.*

Skiles (co-pilot): *Whoa.*

(Sound of thump/thud(s) followed by shuddering sound.)

Skiles: *Oh (expletive).*

Sullenberger: *Oh yeah.*

(Sound similar to decrease in engine noise/frequency begins.)

Skiles: *Uh oh.*

Sullenberger: *We got one rol — both of 'em rolling back.*

(Rumbling sound begins.)

Sullenberger: *Ignition, start.*

Sullenberger: *Mayday mayday mayday. Uh this is uh Cactus fifteen thirty nine hit birds, we've lost thrust (in/on) both engines we're turning back towards LaGuardia.*

LaGuardia departure control: *Ok uh, you need to return to LaGuardia? Turn left heading of uh two two zero.*

(Sound similar to electrical noise from engine igniters begins.)

Skiles: *Airspeed optimum relight. Three hundred knots. We don't have that.*

Sullenberger: *We don't.*

Departure control: *Cactus fifteen twenty nine, if we can get it for you, do you want to try to land runway one three?*

Skiles: *If three nineteen...*

Sullenberger: *We're unable. We may end up in the Hudson.*

Departure control: *Alright Cactus fifteen forty nine it's gonna be left traffic for runway three one.*

Sullenberger: *Unable.*

Departure control: *Okay, what do you need to land?*

Skiles: *(He wants us) to come in and land on one three . . . for whatever.*

Skiles: *FAC (Flight Augmentation Computer) one off, then on.*

Departure control: *Cactus fifteen (twenty) nine runway four's available if you wanna make left traffic to runway four.*

Sullenberger: *I'm not sure we can make any runway. Uh what's over to our right anything in New Jersey maybe Teterboro?*

Departure control: *Ok yeah, off your right side is Teterboro airport.*

Skiles: *No relight after thirty seconds, engine master one and two confirm ...*

Departure control: *You wanna try and go to Teterboro?*

Sullenberger: *Yes.*

Sullenberger *(over public address system): This is the Captain brace for impact.*

Departure control: *Cactus fifteen twenty nine turn right two eight zero, you can land runway one at Teterboro.*

Skiles: *Is that all the power you got? . . . (Wanna) number one? Or we got power on number one.*

Sullenberger: *We can't do it.*

Sullenberger: *Go ahead, try number one.*

Departure control: *Kay which runway would you like at Teterboro?*

Flight Warning Computer: *(Sound of continuous repetitive chime for 9.6 seconds.)*

Sullenberger: *We're gonna be in the Hudson.*

Departure control: *I'm sorry say again Cactus?*

Departure control: *Cactus fifteen forty nine radar contact is lost you also got Newark airport off your two o'clock in about seven miles.*

Skiles: *Got flaps out.*

Skiles: *Two hundred fifty feet in the air.*

Skiles: *Hundred and seventy knots.*

Skiles: *Got no power on either one? Try the other one.*

Radio from another plane: *Two one zero uh forty seven eighteen. I think he said he's going in the Hudson.*

Skiles: *Hundred and fifty knots.*

Skiles: *Got flaps two, you want more?*

Sullenberger: *No let's stay at two.*

Departure control: *Cactus fifteen twenty nine if you can uh....you got uh runway uh two nine available at Newark it'll be two o'clock and seven miles.*

Skiles: *Actually not.*

Sullenberger: *We're gonna brace.*

This was powerful teamwork, orchestrated by an experienced captain who (as he'll tell anyone) was just doing his job. As the plane landed on the Hudson, evacuation began immediately. Inflatable slides and rafts were deployed, and flight attendants led passengers out of the emergency exits. Many passengers were led over seats to avoid rising water. Who was the last person on the plane? Captain Sullenberger. He walked the aisle two final times to check for remaining passengers. All 150 on board survived.

Once again, think back to the heart of the financial crisis in 2008-2009. To quote Warren Buffett, "It's only when the tide goes out do you discover who's been swimming naked." In this environment, Elite Advisors distanced themselves from mediocre advisors. Too many of the latter had been swimming naked, riding the waves of an unprecedented bull market, but now they were exposed.

Howard is a great example of an Elite Advisor. After meeting personally with every affluent client possible, Howard knew he needed to shift gears. He needed to change the focus away from the media drumbeat of doom and gloom and help his clients focus on the positive. It was this train of thought that led Howard to host a series of fun events. These were mostly backyard cookouts with his clients and their families. They grilled burgers and had face painting for the kids.

His invitation list included clients, family members, referral alliance partners and prospects. At first he was a bit leery and thinking, "Should I be promoting a bit of fun and relaxation in the midst of a financial crisis?" Then his true leadership qualities kicked in and he used the financial crisis as a reason to focus on the part of our lives we can control. He wanted to make certain clients didn't let this temporary setback get them down. "Life goes on" became the mantra. Not only did his clients respond favorably, Howard was acquiring new affluent clients from the guests and prospects at his events.

It was around this time that we began coaching Elite Advisors to offer second opinions—and the results were immediate. With eight of ten investors thinking of changing advisors if they encountered a "superior" alternative, we knew that most affluent investors were desperately seeking leadership. They wanted a financial "captain" to guide their families through this mess. An Elite Advisor offering a second opinion was like manna from heaven.

Since most affluent investors have yet to encounter an Elite Advisor who can lead them through these challenging times, the Great Recession has been psychologically and financially damaging, which means that there are still tremendous opportunities for Elite Advisors.

5 Everyday Leadership Traits of Elite Advisors

Our leadership skills are something we need to think about, regardless of the market environment. Most leadership isn't headline-making leadership. Most leadership is the everyday variety that often goes unnoticed. In the financial world, today's investor is looking for trustworthy leadership—someone who can gather and assimilate information, transform that information into knowledge, and offer unbiased advice regarding their family's financial affairs. They want someone who possesses personal integrity, professional competency and a dedicated work ethic.

For financial advisors, leadership manifests itself in many forms:

- *Leading yourself:* Keeping your energy levels high, being a lifelong learner, and being a positive influence on those around you.
- *Leading clients:* Proactively and personally communicating with clients, filtering the noise, and giving them the peace of mind that someone is looking after their family.
- *Leading support personnel:* Keeping morale high, focusing on solutions rather than problems, and instilling a client-first culture.
- *Leading prospects:* Leading them to better financial decisions and helping them understand their options.
- *Leading professional alliances:* maintaining ongoing contact and taking the lead in sharing information.

Elite Advisors excel in delivering everything outlined above, because they take the profession seriously. Yes, Howard was brilliant in adding a little fun to the mix—but he was also tending to his clients' financial needs and concerns. It takes effort to provide leadership to clients, prospects, professional alliances and support personnel. That's why so many advisors found themselves challenged in the Great Recession.

This is fixable, however. With focused effort, leadership is a trait that can be learned and improved over time. Based on our research, advisors would be wise to adopt these five leadership behaviors:

1) **Inspire and direct.** Support staff, team members, strategic referral partners, current clients and affluent prospects must believe that their financial advisor has a strong grasp on today's realities. They need to be assured that their advisor has a plan for the future.
   - Who is someone you've inspired and directed?
   - Who has inspired and directed you? Can you mirror that behavior?
2) **Solve problems.** This is the #1 criterion cited by today's affluent investors when it comes to strengthening loyalty. It's also a quality found in effective leaders. These leaders solve problems quickly and to their clients' satisfaction.
   - What's the last problem that arose for one of your clients?
   - How did you handle it?
   - How did you communicate the solution?
3) **Be open minded.** Change is a constant. Elite Advisors have always been open to new ideas, because they're always looking to the future—their glass is half-full. This is why they're able to meet today's affluent expectations regarding each of the *14 Affluent Commandments.* They are open to making necessary changes.
   - When you're in a conversation about investments, are you open to new ideas?

- What about politics? Do you try to understand others' perspectives?

4) **Be knowledgeable.** In order to inspire and direct, top advisors must develop a healthy capacity for ongoing learning.
   - What is your ongoing process for learning?
   - How much time do you spend reading on a daily basis?
5) **Take risks.** This has nothing to do with investment decisions. We're referring to the psychological risks associated with being wrong. No advisor, not even today's Elite Advisor, is always right. At times, they fail completely. But whether it's communicating a recovery strategy to a current client or selling their services to an affluent prospect, Elite Advisors have the emotional strength to admit mistakes and accept rejection. Most important, they know how to *learn* from their mistakes.
   - What was the last big change you've made in servicing your clients?
   - Do you "play without a net" when prospecting?
   - In Howard's world, scheduling his first family cookout was a risk.

When you come right down to it, the behaviors above describe a financial advisor who knows how to do their job under pressure.

The Leadership Trinity

Most advisors understand the value of being a good leader, but rarely have a structured process to showcase everyday leadership qualities. As is so often the case with good intentions, if our actions aren't systematized and monitored, we tend to be inconsistent. Working to create structure around leadership, we developed a model that reflects what our research uncovered about elite teams. We call it *The Leadership Trinity*:

The Leadership Trinity

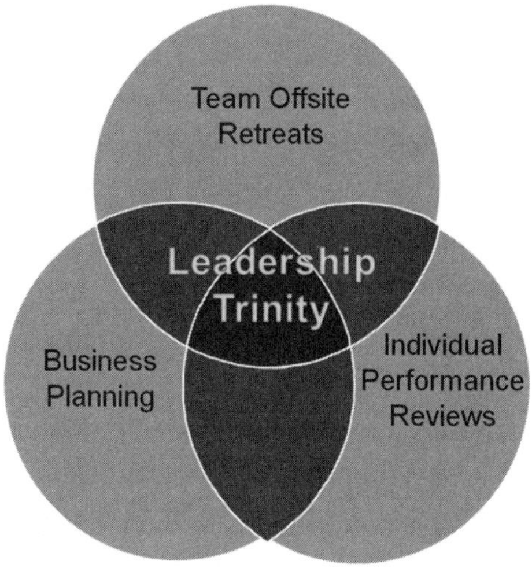

Using these three simple tools, you add structure to things like setting team goals, giving feedback to employees and making strategic plans—things most of us mean to do, but sometimes overlook. The circles in this model overlap because individual performance reviews are based, in part, on measured success in achieving business-plan goals. And the business plan is based on strategies developed at the team's offsite retreat.

Attention "solo" advisors: If you think this model doesn't apply to you, think again. These tools apply whether you have a shared assistant or a team of thirty people. Smaller teams often benefit the most from this advice because they haven't been forced to create this kind of structure in the past.

Team Offsite Retreats

Usually conducted once a year, team offsite retreats provide an opportunity to set goals, reinforce the right culture, and to set metrics for each team member. They also offer an opportunity for having a little fun and getting to know each other on a personal level. Our data shows that only 30% of teams host annual offsite retreats.[15]

When we say "offsite," we mean a meeting that occurs outside a typical office setting. This minimizes the distractions found in the day-to-day environment and emphasizes the importance of the retreat. This is *not* just another meeting.

Bill, an Elite Advisor we've coached, held his team's two-day offsite retreat at his family's beach house. It was about a three hour drive from the office, so all five team members packed up and drove to the coast. Their plan was to have a little fun (they were at the beach after all), to revisit their accomplishments and setbacks from the previous year and to make specific plans for the coming year.

All five team members were given homework assignments regarding team goals, personal goals and roles and responsibilities. Bill led them through a carefully crafted two-day agenda, line item by line item. Each person shared their input and careful notes were taken as action items were discussed.

Most importantly, when the team returned to the office, there was a specific outline of what they had agreed upon. Each person knew the action items for which they were responsible and the team set specific dates to check in on progress. If you asked each team member, they'd tell you this was a valuable experience and well worth the two days out of office.

This was a well-planned, well-executed event, but it's not the only format to consider. We've seen successful offsite retreats hosted on a team member's backyard deck, a private room at the Ritz Carlton, and everything in between. The secret is finding a place that promotes business *and* fun. The length of your offsite retreat will also help determine the location. Some teams opt for a two-hour session while others prefer a three-day affair.

Regardless of the format you choose, we suggest making certain the following components are covered:

- *Team Accountability*
  View this as a performance review for the entire practice. This is where you want everyone accepting their slice of ownership re-

garding annual goals and their individual connection to the team's long-range goals.

- *Individual Accountability*

  Yes, this *is* a bit personal, but only to those who aren't pulling their weight. A team is only as strong as its weakest link, and peer pressure is a strong tonic for performance enhancement. Individual accountability is essential for helping teams realize their potential. Therefore, it's important to review performance standards for each area of responsibility, and develop clear descriptions of those responsibilities—if need be. The idea is to guarantee clear standards for each area. This will enable you to analyze "accountability" in terms of quality, convenience, personalization and value expectations.

  Please note that effective leaders also hold *themselves* accountable. We recently facilitated a retreat at which the team leader spent two hours chastising himself for failing to meet the new asset targets he'd set. Interestingly, everyone else thought he'd done a good job because he'd acquired $90 million of new business. However, his target was $125 million. A good portion of the two hours was spent determining what had held him back, eliciting feedback from team members regarding possible corrective actions, and developing an action plan for the upcoming year.

- *Individual Action Plan*

  An action plan requires everyone to fine-tune their roles, areas of responsibility and performance standards, and then link them to the team's annual goals. Creating action steps should be a component of every performance-based exercise you tackle during the retreat. What you DO NOT want to do is discuss a critical performance issue, keep the conversation at 35,000 feet, and then move to the next agenda item. This will undermine your entire offsite retreat. There should be no grandiose ideas without a practical path to implementation. Effective leaders are very honest when it comes to fine-tuning their roles, reassessing their areas of responsibility and addressing individual performance standards.

- *Brainstorming*
  At some point, venture away from practical matters to facilitate a free-flowing conversation. This is most effective when you select two or three topics, and ask everyone to brainstorm. Ask them to think outside the box (there are no right or wrong ideas), and suggest ideas to improve a particular area. Have one team member serve as the scribe on a white board, writing down an area of improvement, as well as every idea connected to that area. Once you've exhausted everyone's creativity, determine which ideas are actionable, and then prioritize them.

- *Teambuilding*
  This can be done in a number of ways. You can have each team member complete some form of behavioral assessment before the retreat as an ice-breaker for discussion. Or, you can assign a book or magazine article that will be discussed at the retreat. Another exercise generates a lot of laughs and discussion: have everyone list three pieces of personal information that most people don't know about. However, one of these tidbits should be false. Everyone must then guess which nugget of information is fabricated.

- *Communication*
  You should always strive to improve communication among team members. There is no magic formula for improving communication. It's all about being open, honest and respectful of other people's feelings. One exercise could involve going around the table, having each team member share one aspect of communication they do well, and one aspect where they need improvement. Then, encourage everyone else to comment on the good and the bad.

- *Conflict Resolution*
  Stuff happens. People annoy each other from time to time. This is to be expected. However, if there are simmering conflicts, they

should be addressed at the retreat. The following ground rules will help to make this a constructive exercise:

- Identify areas of conflict.
- Input must be constructive.
- Each team member must give input.
- Each team member must provide support for their input.
- Nothing should be on a personal level.
- Agree upon action steps for resolution.

That's it! There's no secret formula for creating a perfect offsite retreat. The only "secret" is conducting the retreats on a regular basis. These retreats are a staple of elite teams, and create a great platform for leadership. Remember: you're treating your practice as a team, even if it's just you and a shared assistant. Offsite retreats, in some form or fashion, are appropriate for *every* financial professional.

Business Planning

The product of every good retreat is an actionable business plan. This plan takes all the great ideas you developed, helps you prioritize them, and guides your efforts throughout the year. The exercise of creating a business plan is facilitated by the team leader, but requires input from everyone. The whole team must buy-in to the plan.

It's been our experience that teams that set up specific times throughout the year to check on their progress are much more likely to stick to their plans. This could be as simple as quarterly checkups for the whole team.

Bill's team organized their action items into a monthly timetable with a monthly meeting to check on progress. They learned from past team offsite retreats that if you create an enormous checklist of action items, without prioritizing or scheduling, you will have some action steps that do not get executed.

We recognize that every business plan is different, but there are some commonalities of successful plans. We suggest incorporating the following to ensure you have a well-crafted, user-friendly business plan:

Envision Your Future

Wouldn't it be great if you could simply look into a crystal ball and see your future business? Actually, you can—or nearly so. Rather than looking toward the future from a historical perspective (this is what I've always done, therefore, this is what I expect to do . . .), you look into your crystal ball (the theater of your mind) and imagine *exactly* what you'd like your practice to look like in five years. Be thorough in your imaging. Imagine the ideal client, the number of ideal clients, the roles of each team member, the scale of your practice, its assets, revenues, etc. Done properly, this step builds a long-range business plan. Think big! (Most people don't.)

Analyze Your Current Business

You'll never reach your goals, no matter how well you imagine your future, without taking inventory of your current business. Analyze your current asset and production levels, the number of clients, new clients added over the past 12 months, clients lost, production growth, asset growth, etc. We also suggest taking a "net profit contribution" inventory of current clients; revenue, assets, as well as potential/current centers-of-influence.

Pay close attention to where your revenue is coming from, potential sources of additional revenue and how many clients fit your minimum and ideal client profiles.

Plan a Structured Marketing Attack

A business that isn't growing is dying. Every business plan should include marketing goals and specific marketing activities designed to help reach those goals. In fact, this should be the focal point of your plan.

Many financial advisors have made marketing too complicated. If you're targeting the affluent, it's all about face-to-face interactions. Remember, the affluent make most of their major decisions, which includes the family's financial affairs, through word-of-mouth influence. Your marketing should be designed to capitalize on this. You need to spend time with top clients, engage in social prospecting, develop professional alliances, etc. It's important to outline your strategy and choose your tactics accordingly.

Define Your Metrics System

Make sure to monitor the right metrics of future success on an annual basis. These metrics include: retention of minimum and ideal clients; number of new ideal clients; number of clients upgraded to minimum and ideal status; new assets; revenue; and the number of smaller clients that have been re-assigned. These statistics will provide an accurate gauge of your progress toward the goals in the business plan. Once your annual targets are defined, we've found it helpful to create quarterly scorecards. (Remember to add a quarterly meeting to your calendar to review your progress.)

Establish Your Fixed Daily Activities (FDAs)

Daily discipline is the price you must pay for success, and you must always pay in advance. This is where the rubber meets the road. FDAs support your Metrics System, and are directly linked to your business plan. For instance, if one of your goals is to strengthen top client relationships, one of your FDAs might be one face-to-face per day with a top client. Done properly, FDAs help ensure that you're on the "critical path" to your envisioned future.

Already have a business plan? Are you using it? We've all seen plans that are created, put on a shelf, and never seen again. Not very helpful! Now is a great time to revisit your business plan as a team.

Individual Performance Reviews

Adherence to the business plan is mandatory and as the team leader, you must inspect what you expect. Individual Performance Reviews provide you this opportunity. The disconnect between advisors and assistants would be hard to match in any other industry. You've heard the refrain:

"My assistant is clueless."
"My FA just doesn't get it."

Our Administrative Assistant research, as we've shared with you earlier in the book, speaks volumes. Assistants feel they're underpaid; advisors feel assistants are overpaid. Assistants feel overworked; advisors see a need for time management. We could go on, but we're guessing you've seen one or two ineffective advisor/assistant relationships.

Communication is the root of most of these issues. How can this be? Advisors talk with their assistants every day, all throughout the day.

There's a big difference between task-related communication and leadership-driven, performance-specific conversation.

Individual performance reviews, scheduled on a regular basis, provide a vehicle for these types of conversations. You're setting aside specific time to address performance in the areas most critical to the role. We know, we know. Many of you have managers who conduct performance reviews with support personnel. We suggest conducting *your own reviews* in addition to whatever reviews the firm conducts. After all, *you* are the one working with this person every day.

The best way to structure the meeting is to create a custom performance-review scorecard for each employee. This sounds like a lot of work, but it's really not. There are three questions that must be answered:

What are the 10 traits that are most important to this position?
Are these completely within the employee's control?
How well is the employee doing in each of these 10 areas?

We've found it helpful to grade this on a 10 point scale: 1 = Poor; 10 = Very Good. Also include a space for both of you to write notes for each of the 10 traits.

When it comes time for performance reviews, the employee and team leader complete the scorecard independently, and then meet to discuss the results. This sets the stage for a very productive meeting—one focused entirely on the 10 most important components of the role.

The following is an example that can help you get started:

1. Communication with team 0 1 2 3 4 5 6 7 8 9 10
   Notes:
2. Communication with clients 0 1 2 3 4 5 6 7 8 9 10
   Notes:
3. Attention to detail 0 1 2 3 4 5 6 7 8 9 10
   Notes:
4. Call/Meeting screening 0 1 2 3 4 5 6 7 8 9 10
   Notes:
5. Task completion 0 1 2 3 4 5 6 7 8 9 10
   Notes:
6. Self-direction 0 1 2 3 4 5 6 7 8 9 10
   Notes:
7. Work ethic 0 1 2 3 4 5 6 7 8 9 10
   Notes:
8. Positive attitude 0 1 2 3 4 5 6 7 8 9 10
   Notes:
9. Prioritization and time management 0 1 2 3 4 5 6 7 8 9 10
   Notes:
10. Personal/professional development 0 1 2 3 4 5 6 7 8 9 10
    Notes:

Frame each meeting as an opportunity to communicate. What's going well and what isn't? At first, support personnel are a bit nervous about these reviews. Over time, if the reviews are conducted properly, they look forward to hearing an update on their performance. It's often been said that people would rather have negative feedback than no feedback at all. There's a lot of truth in that statement.

When planning performance reviews, set a recurring appointment in your calendar and their calendars. Conducting one performance review and then waiting years for another isn't effective. Scheduling them once per quarter can be a game changer.

◆◆◆

Displaying leadership in your day-to-day actions is work—whether it's envisioning things as you would like them to be, communicating this vision to support personnel, or inspecting what you expect. It includes personal accountability, as well as holding your support personnel and junior partners accountable.

Leadership is also quite fragile. Robert is an Elite Advisor who, as of this writing, has been in a coaching relationship with an Oechsli Institute coach for over three years. When he's fully engaged, he leads by example and elevates the performance level of every individual on his team. Robert contacted us about coaching when he realized that his business had plateaued, albeit at a very high level. After completing our Elite Advisor Assessment (an assessment each coaching client must complete), Robert had an epiphany which he shared with his coach:

"I've basically taken the past two years off building my dream house," he said during his initial coaching session. "I was working, but if I'm honest, I probably worked at sixty percent capacity for the past two years. I was always at the building site, micro-managing the contractors, running out of the office to help my wife with minor cosmetic decisions, and expecting my team to carry out my vision without me. I know now that it doesn't work that way. I've got to lead by example. When I'm fully engaged, everyone is fully engaged."

Robert's team averaged $85 million in new assets per year for the past three years, but they're always looking to improve. There were a couple of lulls in this growth that can be directly attributed to extended family vacations in Europe. The difference today is that Robert can *quantify* the impact of his hands-on leadership. He recognizes that this leadership will wane during extended absences, so he communicates this clearly to his team. In addition, expectations during his absence are adjusted, and everyone is willing to follow his lead and work hard in advance of a lengthy vacation, and to do the same on his return. It's not that everyone is goofing-off while Robert is away. On the contrary, because communication is clear, roles and responsibilities are understood, expectations are realistic, everyone is onboard. *This* is leadership.

Leadership is proactive. It rarely can be delegated, and there is nothing casual about it. It's hands-on and personal. Are you ready to lead?

Key Takeaways:

- Leadership is an everyday responsibility of financial advisors; your clients and team members depend on it.
- Many advisors are unstructured in their leadership, which causes inconsistencies.
- The Leadership Trinity includes team offsite retreats, business planning and individual performance reviews. All three work together.
- Fixed Daily Activities help make your business planning actionable.
- Individual performance reviews are essential in inspecting what you expect.

8

Lifelong Learning

"An investment in knowledge pays the best interest."

- Benjamin Franklin

Benjamin Franklin taught himself the printing business. Steve Jobs schooled himself on electronics. Howard Shultz learned the coffee business. Each of these elite performers mastered his profession after "school was out."

In reality, school is never "out" for the elite performer. As Charlie Munger once wrote, "In my whole life, I have known no wise people who didn't read all the time—none, zero. You'd be amazed at how much Warren [Buffett] reads—and at how much I read. My children laugh at me, they think I'm a book with a couple of legs sticking out."[16]

Charlie Munger isn't alone. Listen to the value that other elite performers ascribed to learning and reading:

> *Steve Jobs*: "Until recently when Steve Jobs of Apple sold his collection, he reportedly had an 'inexhaustible interest' in the books of William Blake—the mad visionary 18th-century mystic poet and artist."

> *Elizabeth I*: "The empire-loving Elizabeth I surrounded herself with the Roman historians, many of whom she translated, and kept one book under lock and key in her bedroom, in a French translation she alone of her court could read: Machiavelli's treatise on how to overthrow republics, 'The Prince.'"

> *Winston Churchill:* "Churchill retreated to his library to heal his wounds after being voted out of power in 1945—and after reading for six years came back to power."
>
> "It took Dee Hock, father of the credit card and founder of Visa, a thousand books to find The One. Mr. Hock walked away from business life in 1984 and looked back only from his library's walls."[17]

"Reading can also make you more effective in leading others. Reading increases verbal intelligence, making a leader a more adept and articulate communicator. Reading novels can improve empathy and understanding of social cues, allowing a leader to better work with and understand others—traits that author Anne Kreamer persuasively linked to increased organizational effectiveness, and to pay raises and promotions for the leaders who possessed these qualities. And any business person understands that heightened emotional intelligence will improve his or her leadership and management ability."[18]

"If you look at our data and the data of other studies, you are almost compelled to believe that there is now a bifurcation in the American population between one group, which takes an active stance towards managing their own lives, and another group, which is increasingly passive. The passive people come home, watch TV, play video games, go onto the Internet, talk on the phone, go back to the TV, put a DVD in—and then it's time to go to bed. What you see for the first time in American history is that less than half of the U.S. adult American population is reading literature."[19]

This is a major societal trend that should prompt everyone to think critically about the direction of our young people. How will a decrease in lifelong learning affect their ability to compete globally? How will we manage a generation that seems more comfortable texting than talking?

You might also be wondering, "What does this have to do with being an Elite Advisor?" Plenty. Here's the linkage:

1) Leading Your Clients

Your ability to gather, filter and disseminate information is essential to being perceived as a knowledge worker instead of someone who recites the "company line." In today's new world, with information bombarding the affluent 24/7, your role as someone able to cut through the white noise and separate fact from fiction, positions you as not just a trusted source of information, but as someone who is indispensable.

Elite Advisors:

- Share specific and timely information with clients, cutting through the white noise.
- Avoid data dumping, realizing that less information, carefully sifted, is more impactful.
- Speak intelligently (and intelligibly) about world and economic events; avoiding industry jargon.
- Break down complex ideas into simple terms that can be understood by those outside of the financial services industry.
- Keep clients on track by helping them tune out information sources that are counterproductive to their financial goals.
- Share books with clients when appropriate. Howard, the Elite Advisor who hosted the fun events during the financial crisis, also shared books with his clients (i.e. *The Snowball* by Alice Schroeder). In his words, "Even if the clients don't read the book, they appreciate the thought and it reinforces the fact that I'm well-read." Another tip—always read the books that you are sending.

2) Building Rapport

People who are well-read on a variety of topics are usually good conversationalists, as long as they also have good people skills. Elite Advisors possess both attributes, which helps them to be at ease when connecting with people. This is priceless when dealing with today's affluent.

Put simply: as a lifelong learner, you increase your ability to talk with people about things that interest *them,* while at the same time being interesting yourself. If you're talking with someone who loves to go hiking, and you've just read an article about a new trail *and* you're fairly knowledgeable about the environment, you have a leg-up in developing rapport. If you're talking with someone whose hobby is collecting historical miniatures, and you have a working knowledge of history that allows you to ask sincere questions and proactively listen to the responses, you have a leg-up in developing rapport.

Elite Advisors:

- Showcase their knowledge by making subtle references to books and articles, rather than sitcoms and celebrities. However, you do not want to come across as a know-it-all.
- Find areas of commonality by uncovering their interests, allowing them to showcase *their* knowledge. Talk about what's important to them; *their* passions.
- Hold other people's interest by being a good conversationalist and a proactive listener.
- Acquire personal *and* professional respect by possessing a wide breadth of knowledge.

Elite Advisors are constantly working to build their knowledge base. They have an insatiable curiosity, which fuels their thirst for knowledge. They want to stay current, and they are always gathering more information, but they use the information carefully. Elite Advisors don't take over conversations just because they've just read a book connected to the discussion. They don't send clients a daily digest of market information to appear smart. They interject bits of knowledge and information as needed, whether to move a conversation along or keep a client informed.

3) Depth & Breadth of Industry Knowledge

One of the *14 Affluent Commandments* is *depth and breadth of industry knowledge.* Affluent clients not only want the advisor to be a lifelong learner, but to also be a lifetime student of their chosen profession. They want their advisor to be smart, up-to-date and ahead of the curve. Elite Advisors personify this characteristic.

We're seeing veteran advisors investing time, energy and money to expand their knowledge base. William is a great example. He's an Ivy League grad, has earned his CFA (certified financial analyst) designation, and is a master rainmaker.

Before William mastered rainmaking, however, he was spending all of his time using his CFA brain to manage his client's money. He was good at it, but had little time for anything else. He was also a voracious reader, devouring two to three books a month. William didn't read fiction. His reading consisted mostly of biographies of famous people, serious business books and history. Not only was he well-read and a great conversationalist, he had an epiphany while reading Ron Chernow's *The Titan* (a biography of John D. Rockefeller, Sr.)—realizing that he needed to learn how to delegate if he wanted to reach his potential. This led William far outside his comfort zone on a laborious journey of hiring a CFA who could perform day-to-day analysis while following William's guidelines. Five years later, William has three CFAs on his team, which has freed him to bring in more than $600 million of new money. Previously, he averaged $15 million to $20 million of new money per year, a figure many advisors would consider outstanding, but not William. Why not? William amplified his ambition through studying his role models, which were acquired from his thirst for learning. Although John D. Rockefeller, Sr. was one,Warren Buffet was his primary role model.

Role Models

William is not an isolated example. Behind every high achiever is usually a positive role model. This is an integral part of lifelong learning. Think of this role model as a mentor, hero, confidant, mother, father...the label isn't important. It's simply important to realize that, throughout recorded history, significant personal and professional growth has often been stimulated by identifying with—and emulating—a role model.

Do you have a hero? Do you have a role model? Most people have none. Could this be why so few people scratch the surface of their God-given potential? We think it merits serious consideration.

In school, rote learning is emphasized and rewarded in the safe structured environment. Not in the real world. Acquired role-model habits make the difference between knowledge and performance.

Case Study #1:	Michael Jordan
Claim to Fame:	Basketball Superstar
Role Models:	David Thompson and Walter Davis

Michael Jordan patterned his game after two local basketball heroes, David Thompson and Walter Davis. He watched their games on TV, and read about them whenever possible. They were his inspiration to excel, to dunk, and to make it to the NBA.

Case Study #2:	General George Patton
Claim to Fame:	Military Leader Extraordinaire
Role Model:	Alexander the Great

General George Patton idolized Alexander the Great. As a youth, he studied everything ever written about his hero. When General Patton was in the heat of battle against the Nazis in Europe, all of his decisions were made with consideration of how his role model, Alexander, would have acted under similar circumstances. A cynic might say it's a coincidence that neither general lost a battle, but we respectfully disagree.

In the spaces that follow, identify two heroes. This might not be easy if you've never had a hero. Just think about two people with whom you would gladly trade places. Dead or alive, it makes no difference. After identifying these heroes, list six qualities and characteristics that contributed to their greatness. These can be everyday qualities such as confidence, discipline, etc. Here's a brief example:

Hero 1: Ben Franklin

Major Accomplishments: One of the Founding Fathers of the USA

Noted author, politician, inventor, entrepreneur

Qualities and Characteristics:

1. Disciplined
2. Industrious
3. Practical

4. Honest
5. Persistent
6. Goal-focused

Hero 1: ______________________________

Major Accomplishments: ______________________________

Qualities and Characteristics:

1. ______________________________
2. ______________________________
3. ______________________________
4. ______________________________
5. ______________________________
6. ______________________________

Hero 2: ______________________________

Major Accomplishments: ______________________________

Qualities and Characteristics:

1. ______________________________
2. ______________________________
3. ______________________________
4. ______________________________
5. ______________________________
6. ______________________________

Inner Qualities vs. School Qualities

Now that you've identified qualities and characteristics of greatness in your heroes, it's time to label these as inner qualities (IQ'S) or school qualities (SQ'S). Use the following as your working definitions for this exercise:

INNER QUALITIES (IQ's): Qualities and characteristics that have been developed through life experience. These are attributable to living and growing outside of the classroom.

SCHOOL QUALITIES (SQ's): This is textbook knowledge—information you were fed by a teacher in a classroom, and tested on. Much product knowledge is SQ, along with your ability to spell.

There will be some overlap as you label your heroes' traits. This is only natural. When this happens, assign the most dominant label to the quality. Upon completion of the labeling, compare the percentage of inner qualities to school qualities—IQ'S versus SQ's.

Hero 1:
Inner Qualities _______
School Qualities _______
percent of IQ's _______

Hero 2:
Inner Qualities _______
School Qualities _______
percent of IQ's _______

In many workshops, we've been amazed at how many participants label 100 percent of their heroes' qualities and characteristics as *inner qualities*!

Did you list a Ph.D. from Harvard or Yale as a major contributor? How about a college education? Probably not.

People are taken back by the requirements, in their own estimation, for high-level achievement. Most of these requirements are not taught in a classroom. Most do not require genius-level intelligence.

What's encouraging to financial professionals, as we teach these principles throughout the country, is that the opportunity for high-level achievement is available for all who are willing. All of those inner qualities are very natural, and can be developed by taking control of your internal tapes and self-image. It's simple, but not easy. This is the essence of winning the inner game of selling.

Adding Structure

Whether you're an active learner or haven't picked up a book in years, we'd like to share some helpful tools for building your knowledge base. A real commitment to lifelong learning doesn't mean picking up a book every so often or skimming a few websites. It requires an ongoing and structured quest for knowledge.

When thinking about structured learning, we often think about the university system. It's a well-organized and proven system for building knowledge. Its structure is a big reason for its effectiveness. Students are provided with a specific list of courses to take, assignments to complete and materials to read.

If you went back to school as an adult, the structure would impact your mindset. You'd be thinking about how to juggle your schedule, when to do homework, how to prepare for the exams, and so on. You would be mentally "engaged," and would make the most of your experience. You'd go to class regularly, do the required studying and finish your degree brimming with new knowledge—all because of the structure.

How can we elicit the same commitment and engagement without going back to school?

Structure for You

A learning plan is a great place to start. Like a business plan, a learning plan is a written document outlining your learning goals and specific areas of interest in a structured format. This plan isn't handed to you by a college professor or a manager. This is *your* plan—a personal one created by you.

Most learning plans include the following components:

Objective (what you want to learn and how you plan to learn about it):

Example: To deepen my knowledge about alternative investments, Civil War history and elder law through morning study sessions and nightly reading.

To-Learn List (a list of topics you'd like to learn more about):

Example:

- Private equity
- Venture capital
- Art as an investment
- Abraham Lincoln

- General Lee
- General Grant
- Dementia
- Assisted living facilities

Structure of Studying:

- 7–8:00 a.m.—Reading, note-taking and filing (online, magazines, etc.)
- 9–10 p.m.—Book reading

Lesson Plans (the plan for the next thing on the "To-Learn" list):

Private Equity:

- Schedule a lunch with XYZ person (expert on alternative investments)
- Read XYZ book from Amazon
- Read weekly newsletter from XYZ source
- Find sources on history of private equity (introduction of LBO, etc.)

That's it. All it takes is a pen and paper and an hour or two of alone time, and you'll have a customized learning plan. If done properly and kept in plain sight, it's an indispensable personal guide to lifelong learning.

Structure for Clients

The clients of Elite Advisors don't plug into flavor-of-the-month, stock-of-the-minute TV or radio programs. Why? They know their advisors will keep them informed of anything that might impact their portfolios. When the markets take a turn, or a new law is passed, their advisor is calling to let them know what's happening and to recommend appropriate changes.

Don't forget that one of the *14 Affluent Commandments* is *proactive contact.* This is a big deal. The consequences of failure are grim. Clients can tune-out or, worse, they will tune-in somewhere else.

The most common information-sharing mistakes include:

- *Overload.* The advisor understands the need to be an information source, but goes overboard; sending too many messages, too mechanically. The clients tune out without personal instruction.
- *Sales Bias.* Every contact has a "hook"— i.e., "Here's a great article about the rising cost of nursing home facilities. Did you know we offer long-term care insurance?"
- *Inconsistency.* The client rarely hears from the advisor. Maybe an occasional newsletter or a random phone call, but not enough for positioning as a trusted information source.

The goal is to become a consistent and trusted source of information. This means regular phone calls, as well as sending newsletters and articles when appropriate. But be careful about mixing sales with information.

If you want to gauge your effectiveness as a trusted source of information, run the following drill. In your next round of client reviews, end your meeting with a couple of questions: "Where else are you getting financial information? Are there newspapers, TV programs or people who provide this information?"

Your objective is two-fold:

1. You want to learn if they're tuning into news sources that are counterproductive to their financial health. This gives you a chance to explain that XYZ TV show can be entertaining, but their strategy is very different than our current plan.
2. You want to learn if clients have friends, family members or colleagues with whom they discuss financial issues. What better introduction could there be?

Positioning yourself as a trusted information source happens one interaction at a time, over time. What call could you make to top clients this week? What personal email might you send?

Learning Resources

Recommended Reading List

Matt has often been asked to put out a recommended reading list. While everyone's reading list reflects their interests and passions, it's always great to pick up a book that's highly recommended. The following list is by no means complete, but it's a great start:

1. *Management Challenges for the 21st Century*—by Peter Drucker
2. *Steve Jobs: The Exclusive Biography*—by Walter Isaacson
3. *Built to Last*—by Jim Collins
4. *Good to Great*—by Jim Collins
5. *The Art of Living*—by Epictetus
6. *The Marketing Imagination*—by Theodore Levitt
7. *The Real Warren Buffett*—by James O'Loughlin
8. *The Snowball*—by Alice Schroeder
9. *The Autobiography of Benjamin Franklin*—by Benjamin Franklin
10. *The First American; The Life and Times of Benjamin Franklin*—By H.W. Brands
11. *Alexander Hamilton*—by Ron Chernow
12. *The Millionaire Next Door*—by Thomas Stanley
13. *1776*—by David McCullough
14. *His Excellency: George Washington*—by Joseph Ellis
15. *Founding Brothers*—by Joseph Ellis
16. *Seeking Wisdom; From Darwin to Munger*—by Pete Bevelin
17. *The Endurance*—by Caroline Alexander
18. *The World is Flat*—by Tom Friedman
19. *Outliers*—by Malcolm Gladwell
20. *Relationship Marketing*—by Regis McKenna
21. *Leading Minds; An Anatomy of Leadership*—by Howard Gardner
22. *Golf in the Kingdom*—by Michael Murphy
23. *Peak Performance*—by Charles Garfield

24. *Psycho-Cybernetics*—by Maxwell Maltz
25. *Think and Grow Rich*—by Napoleon Hill
26. *How to Win Friends and Influence People*—by Dale Carnegie
27. *Grinding it Out*—by Ray Kroc
28. *Made in America*—by Sam Walton
29. *Becoming a Rainmaker*—by Matt Oechsli
30. *Head First: The Biology of Hope*—by Norman Cousins
31. *The Art of War*—by Sun Tzu (edited & forward by James Clavell)
32. *The Inner Athlete*—by Robert Neideffer
33. *The Power of Habit*—by Charles Duhigg
34. *Leading Minds*—by Howard Gardner
35. *Extraordinary Minds*—by Howard Gardner
36. *Team of Rivals*—by Doris Kearns Goodwin
37. *Positioning*—by Al Ries and Jack Trout
38. *The Path of Least Resistance*—by Robert Fritz
39. *Conceptual Selling*—by Robert Miller and Stephen Heiman
40. *Extraordinary Golf: The Art of the Possible*—by Fred Shoemaker
41. *Titan*—by Ron Chernow
42. *The Psychology of Influence*—by Robert Cialdini
43. *The Experience Economy*—by Joseph Pine II and James Gilmore
44. *The Affluent Handbook*—by Matt Oechsli
45. *How I Raised Myself from Failure to Success in Selling*—by Frank Bettger
46. *The Big Short*—by Michael Lewis
47. *Liar's Poker*—by Michael Lewis
48. *Partners in Command*—by Mark Perry
49. *Julius Caesar*—by Philip Freeman
50. *Rome 1960*—by David Maraniss

Education 2.0

In today's digital age, education is at your fingertips. What's more: it's free! We all know the Internet is loaded with articles, whitepapers and podcasts. The Internet has gone from a novelty to a powerful and ubiquitous force.

One Internet learning tool has been attracting a lot of attention lately—the free online classes offered by top universities.

"Online classes have been around for years, with technology evolving to include multimedia features and interaction among students and faculty. What is new is the way top colleges are jumping in with free courses — in effect, throwing open the doors digitally."[20]

Schools like Stanford, MIT, Duke, University of Pennsylvania, Harvard and Princeton are all offering free classes on the Web. The renowned author of *Predictable Irrational*, Dan Ariely from Duke University, teaches a class on "Irrational Behavior." You can learn about great topics from top talent, and get real-life homework assignments.

The classes don't count toward a degree, but that's not the focus here anyway. We're pursuing lifelong learning. Whether you're looking for insights on the human brain, the fundamentals of running a small business or the history of the world, there's something for everyone.

Whether it's online learning, reading a book, or mirroring a role model, learning is a process that should never stop. Virtually every elite business, political, military and spiritual leader has been an avid reader, thinker and learner. It makes them who they are. Care to join them?

Key Takeaways:

- Elite Advisors are knowledge workers and always looking to learn new things.
- To learn consistently, you need to create a process. This could involve morning reading, spending time with a mentor/role model, etc.
- Role models are important in developing the right habits. The quickest way to mirror their success is by mirroring their habits.
- Pick up a good biography from our Recommended Reading list. Reading about great success stories helps light those internal fires of motivation.
- Read one good book every three months (one per quarter).
- Send one good book to your clients once a year (one that you have read!)

9

Balance

Factoid: The majority of financial advisors, 62.7%, get 0–3 days of exercise per week.[12]

December 2008: "I just can't take much more of this. The phones are ringing off the hook. I'm trying to stay on top of what's happening with the markets. My team has been in a panic. Something's gotta give."

This was a common conversation we had with advisors during the depths of the financial crisis. Clients were worried about their portfolios, advisors were worried about their portfolios (and income), and everyone was sailing downriver on a seemingly rudderless ship.

While we can be certain that managing expectations and making outbound contact before this volatile period would have lowered stress levels to some degree for advisors and clients, this wasn't the course of action for many.

Hence, more panicked calls came in, more meetings were scheduled, and more time was spent in the office. Worse, advisors spent most of this time playing defense. Very little attention was paid to client acquisition during what was arguably the best period for client acquisition in our lifetimes. For many advisors, the extra time required to soothe the fears of spooked clients was so taxing that it borrowed from family, friends and physical activity. The result: high levels of stress for everyone involved.

The Great Recession aside, financial services professionals have always been challenged when it comes to work-life balance. After all, success is all about making money, right? You know the Wall Street mantra: it's all about the money. Get it while you can. You can always kick back and enjoy the fruits of your labors once you've made your millions. Ouch! It hurts just *thinking* about that myopic approach, but this has been the reality for many advisors.

In any business in which effort dictates the size of the paycheck, there's a risk of overdoing it. It wasn't long ago that pounding the phones all day was a legitimate path to the corner office, but the days of the chain-smoking, heavy-drinking, sedentary advisor are over.

One of the biggest myths is that today's Elite Advisor is a work-addicted, family-neglecting egomaniac. That's simply not the case. Elite Advisors work hard, but their success is largely determined by what they *do* with their work hours. They work smart.

What we discovered was not really a surprise: Elite Advisors make it a priority to maintain a healthy degree of balance in their lives. They're physically active, spend quality time with their families, and are stewards of their communities. We've often asked Elite Advisors for copies of their schedules—daily, weekly and monthly. We're always amazed at how busy, and yet productive, they are. It reminds us of the adage, "If you want to get something done, give the task to a busy person."

Reviewing their schedules not only helps us help them; it provides us with a model for other advisors to follow. There's usually not a dull spot in their agenda. From time spent reading the newspaper, to exercise, to client appointments, to committee meetings, to meals with their families, these advisors stay active.

A few years ago, we conducted a psychographic affluent study. With all the press devoted to the demographics associated with affluent baby-boomers, we wanted to get behind the curtain to gain insight to how they made decisions, and what motivated their decision-making. What we discovered were four psychographic motivators that influenced how they lived their lives, personally and professionally. We refer to them as the four key motivators:

- Personal health
- Family health

- Financial health
- Spiritual health

These four key motivators determine the context of the priorities they establish, the decisions they make, and their personal and professional actions. Elite Advisors operate within the same framework. After all, they're also affluent. Let's take a look at each of these motivators.

Family Health

Although they don't spend every evening at the dinner table, Elite Advisors' families *do* come first. They are extremely busy, but still make it a priority to attend their children's (or grandkids') ballgames, and enjoy meals with their spouses. These activities are calendared and prioritized in much the same way that affluent client activities are scheduled. Because family is a priority, family relationships also benefit from a structured approach to relationship management.

Here's a brief sampling of an Elite Advisor's family schedule:

Monday:	Home with family.
Tuesday:	Client/referral alliance/prospect dinner.
Wednesday:	Daughter's soccer game.
Thursday:	Socializing after work, home late.
Friday:	Date night (dinner and a movie with the spouse).
Saturday:	Office or business golf (morning), activity with the kids (afternoon).
Sunday:	Family day.

Whether it's a Sunday dinner, Thanksgivings at the beach or nighttime walks with the dog, Elite Advisors make time for family. For them, what matters is the quality, not quantity, of time.

Financial Health

Elite Advisors lead by example and are usually found living inconspicuously and within their means. The idea of buying the biggest house you can't afford, and selling your way into affordability is yesterday's news. Elite Advisors aren't ashamed of their success, but they're also not buying the biggest house in town or driving the biggest Mercedes on the market. The old saying, "it's hard to teach what you don't do" holds true. Helping clients make smart financial decisions starts by making smart financial decisions yourself.

Spiritual Health

Although fewer people attend structured religious services than ever before in our history,[21] the affluent investor, as well as Elite Advisors, are still driven by their spiritual beliefs. It's not our place to offer advice on spirituality. We're simply making the case that balance—taking time to maintain all areas of your life—is an important trait of Elite Advisors.

Personal Health

The personal health business is booming in the United States. Yet the US is riddled with health issues—childhood obesity, inadequate health care coverage, sedentary lifestyles, and the list goes on. It's not that we're getting healthier, it's that we're focusing more on health. Our research shows a clear divide within the ranks of advisors—those who consistently find time for physical activity and those who don't. Let's take a moment to explore this in more detail.

Fitness and Elite Advisors

"I start my day with exercise—every day. And I insist that other members of our group take time to stay in shape as well," said Sam during one of our Rainmaker Focus Group sessions. This was an interesting comment—one that sparked a lengthy conversation about the relationship between personal fitness and Rainmaking.

Not every participant of this elite group was a triathlete or long-distance runner, but they all made time in their day for some form of exercise, even if it was walking the dog early in the morning. Some exercised in the morning, others exercised over lunch, and others got it done after work. Contrast this with the industry as a whole:

Average Days Per Week of Exercise	
0-3	62.7 percent
4	13.8 percent
5	15.3 percent
6	3 percent
7	5.2 percent

Oechsli Institute Financial Advisor Research[12]

According to our research, 62.7 percent of advisors aren't getting the exercise they need. From this, we can deduce that more than half of financial advisors don't have the energy necessary for elite performance.

No matter your level of current fitness, there's always work to be done. We find that physical fitness plays into running an elite practice in two ways:

Creating Energy for Running Your Business

As everyone from our Rainmaker Focus Group can attest, it takes serious energy to run a financial practice. You're basically working three full time jobs—servicing clients, finding new clients and managing your family and social life. This can (and does) lead to career burn out. The best advisors, new advisors and veterans alike, achieve balance in their life. They know that dedicating an hour a day to personal health makes the rest of their day more productive.

Here are some ways to increase your energy levels:

- Exercise 30 minutes a day, five days a week (as recommended by the American Heart Association).
- Eat nutritious meals, and snack on healthy foods throughout the day. We all know the feeling of having a big lunch then feeling sluggish all afternoon. This can be avoided.
- Try standing up for phone calls. It not only keeps your blood flowing, it makes you sound more alive. We know one top advisor who works from a standing desk to make certain he sounds alert and energized.

Building Your Network through Exercise

Why not work on your business while you work on your body? There are so many ways to use exercise for Rainmaking. You can exercise with a partner, find a group that shares your exercise routine (walking, running, swimming), or even take group exercise classes at your gym. These are all great ways to meet people with similar passions.

We've heard many instances of new business coming from the gym, but we've also known many advisors who exercise heavily and bring in very little business. Here are some tips to maximize the client acquisition aspect of your workouts:

1. Find the right club/activity that attracts regulars who fit your ideal client profile. If a certain class at the gym attracts a different group of people for every class, or if it's full of college students, you may have trouble developing the right relationships.

   Imagine landing a physician client as a result of a forty-mile Saturday morning group cycling ride. That's exactly what happened to an advisor we coached. After getting to know this physician through cycling and transforming him into a client advocate, he landed *seven additional physicians over a nine month period!* And it all started with a little exercise—a bike ride.
2. Exercise at the right times. If your target market includes corporate execs, you'll want to select a group that meets early in the morning, over lunch or after work. If you're looking for retirees, mid-morning might be perfect.
3. Plan how you'll convert social contacts to business contacts. The social prospecting process works by meeting new people, developing relationships with them, and ultimately asking them to do business with you. Each of these steps must happen to successfully bring in new business. As you get to know people—and they find out what you do—they're likely to ask market-related questions. *These* are your windows of opportunity to offer your services!

4. Take a few minutes longer to exercise. If you're rushing through your workout and rushing to get back to the office, you're probably missing some great interactions with other members.
5. Consider an intimate event built around exercise. You could bring in a nutritionist to talk about keeping your body healthy, then share a few thoughts on keeping your portfolio healthy as well. Or you could host an event around a certain client interest—e.g., if you have lots of cyclists, organize a long ride for a Saturday morning. The possibilities are endless.

Elite Advisors are always hunting for ways to broaden their community footprint. Exercise is not only an excellent way to do this; it's a great way to maintain your energy and sanity during tough times. Since *you* are the product, and first impressions are lasting, being in shape (which allows you to look and feel good) has a major impact on your personal brand.

Maintaining Work-Life Balance

We all find ourselves out of balance from time to time—not spending enough time at home, not spending enough time at work, or not getting enough exercise. Well, recognition is half of recovery. Once you've identified a deficiency in one of these areas, it's time for some self-reflection to determine a more effective way to manage your time.

During times of crisis, stress and imbalance are often unavoidable. That's OK. Our energy is best spent on making the most of a "typical" week. We often recommend a two-week time/motion study. This is tedious, but effective. Here's the drill:

1. Print a weekly calendar (search online for "blank weekly calendar," and you'll find hundreds).
2. Keep exact records of what you're doing during each hour of the day.
3. Conduct this exercise over a two-week period.
4. Analyze your results.

The results of this exercise are different for everyone. Are you spending too much time on small clients? Could you be more efficient with your first hour in the office? Are you spending too much time in the office?

If you find that your work-life balance is out of whack, the following are some work-life balance tips from the Mayo Clinic. They've dealt with work stress for decades, and offer some great advice:

> ***"Learn to say no.*** Whether it's a co-worker asking you to spearhead an extra project or your child's teacher asking you to organize a class party, remember that it's OK to respectfully say "no." When you quit accepting tasks out of guilt or a false sense of obligation, you'll have more time for the activities that are meaningful to you.
>
> ***Track your time.*** Pay attention to your daily tasks, including work-related and personal activities. Decide what's necessary and what satisfies you most. Eliminate or delegate activities you don't enjoy or can't handle, or share your concerns and possible solutions with your employer or others.
>
> ***Manage your time.*** Organize household tasks efficiently, such as running errands in batches or doing a load of laundry every day, rather than saving it all for your day off. Put family events on a weekly family calendar, and keep a daily to-do list. Do what needs to be done; let the rest go.
>
> ***Nurture yourself.*** Eat a healthy diet, include physical activity in your daily routine and get enough sleep. Set aside time each day for an activity that you enjoy, such as practicing yoga or reading. Better yet, discover activities you can do with your partner, family or friends—such as hiking, dancing or taking cooking classes."[22]

These tips are timeless. The next time you're feeling overly stressed, take a step back and run our time/motion study. You'll likely find there are two or three things you can delegate, stop doing, or do differently. A few fine tunings can make all the difference.

Key Takeaways:

- Elite Advisors work hard, but they balance their time between work, friends, family and community.
- Physical fitness helps you maintain the energy you need to operate at high levels. It's hard to be as active as an Elite Advisor if your endurance is low.
- Join an exercise group or class as part of your business development efforts. Walking, running or group fitness classes are great ways to meet new people.
- Take time out for yourself. If you don't take control of your schedule and allow for rest and relaxation, nobody will.
- Help your clients lead balanced lifestyles. Host intimate events for top clients around personal fitness, work/life balance or other pertinent topics.

Conclusion

Back in 1954, a milkshake machine salesman visited the first McDonald's restaurant in San Bernardino, California. He wanted to know why they needed eight expensive milkshake machines when most other restaurants needed one. He was blown away by the level of business being done by such a simple operation. They only sold hamburgers, cheeseburgers, fries, milkshakes and sodas. There was no wait staff and very simple decor. He surveyed several people on site and found that many of them were visiting the restaurant every single day. Ray Kroc, former Multimixer salesman, couldn't sleep that night as his mind filled with visions of McDonald's, the new American institution, running through his mind.

Where would Ray Kroc's ambition take him today if he were a financial advisor? One could only envision that he (or any other notable business icon) would see the current opportunity for acquiring more affluent clients. He would have the discipline to source names, attend affluent social events, and get personally introduced to potential clients. If he found himself awkward in affluent social circles, he'd have the self-awareness to recognize this weakness and correct it.

This is exactly how Elite Advisors responded to the Great Recession. For them, it's been a perfect storm of opportunity. As we analyzed our findings, it became apparent that Elite Advisors possess four qualities—personality traits so delicately woven into their character that they are practically part of their DNA. These qualities, as evidenced in Ray Kroc, are ambition, discipline, self-awareness and deliberate practice. Take a few minutes to assess where you stand. This self-assessment is based on a 1 to 5 scale, with 1 = dormant and 5 = fully engaged.

Please be honest with your assessment, and describe how you can fully activate that trait.

1. *Ambition.* You never have to help an Elite Advisor think big. Whether grandiose thinking is in their DNA or they developed it

along the way, Elite Advisors are big thinkers. They are the advisors who are able to imagine their future, see things that aren't there, and set what Jim Collins of *Good to Great* calls "big hairy audacious goals."

Be honest, and rate your current level of ambition using the 1 to 5 scale below.

1 2 3 4 5

Action Step: ________________________________

2. *Discipline.* This trait is so often used in the mundane sense of developing good habits (eating right, exercising or working smart) that its value is frequently overlooked. The kind of discipline we have in mind is the sort specifically linked to goals. If an Elite Advisor needs to attend a social function (i.e. silent auction to raise money for one of his affluent client's charities), he attends that event, even if he'd rather be home watching the ball game. Elite Advisors have the discipline to do what must be done, even when they'd rather be doing something else.

   Be honest, and rate your current level of discipline using the 1 to 5 scale below.

   1 2 3 4 5

   Action Step: ________________________________

3. *Self-Awareness.* To borrow Malcolm Gladwell's phrase "tipping point," this trait is the tipping point between Elite Advisors and the garden-variety "good advisor." Because of their ambition, Elite Advisors hold themselves to extremely high standards, which causes them to be very critical of themselves and others. This makes them acutely aware of any weaknesses that could interfere with their ambition. They recognize that these shortcomings, left unchecked, will keep them from achieving their dreams. Non-elite advisors rationalize why their weaknesses aren't very important instead of identifying

and correcting them. As a result, they tend to get defensive about their weaknesses and focus on only their strengths.

Be honest, and rate your current level of self-awareness using the 1 to 5 scale below.

1 2 3 4 5

Action Step: ____

4. *Deliberate Practice.* Once performance-specific weaknesses are identified, Elite Advisors work to correct them. This type of focused attention is known as "deliberate practice" by behavioral psychologists. You see this trait in elite athletes in every sport. Whether it was basketball legend Michael Jordan working to become a top defender, or tennis great Rafael Nadal putting in countless hours of practice to improve his serve, the greats do the hard work that's needed to correct performance-specific weaknesses. For many advisors, deliberate practice takes the form of mastering affluent sales skills. For others, it's about learning to delegate, while still others need to develop leadership skills. Whatever the performance-specific weakness, Elite Advisors do whatever it takes to transform weaknesses into strengths.

   Be honest, and rate your current level of deliberate practice using the 1 to 5 scale below.

   1 2 3 4 5

   Action Step: ____

We know that some people still buy in to the "old school" of thought. They believe that Elite Advisors are born, not made. We respectfully disagree. We've had the good fortune of observing these qualities in advisors *as they were being developed.*

From our collective 40 years of performance coaching, as well as numerous independent research projects on elite performers, we've learned that every financial advisor who makes a personal commitment to model Elite Advisors can develop these four traits.

We're going to assume that you're ambitious, as you've hung in there with us chapter after chapter to the end. This also is a good indicator that you have the discipline necessary to be an Elite Advisor. Keep up the hard work!

Elite Advisor status is possible for every financial professional, regardless of background, personality type, or natural sales ability. With the right focus and dedication, BIG results are possible.

Sources

1. Oechsli Institute (2013). Understanding the Affluent. n=465 with $250,000 to $10,000,000 investable assets
2. Oechsli Institute (2013). Affluent Focus Groups. $500,000 to $10,000,000 in investable assets
3. Oechsli Institute and Nationwide Financial (2012). Affluent Investor Study. n=400 with $250,000 to $10,000,000 investable assets
4. Oechsli Institute (2013). Elite Financial Advisors. n=721 advisors from multiple distribution channels
5. Christakis, Nicholas A., Fowler, James H., Connected: The Surprising Power of Our Social Networks and How They Shape Our Lives. New York: Little, Brown and Company, 2009.
6. Oechsli Institute and Cetera Financial (2011). Marketing Tactics of Elite Advisors. n=352 advisors from multiple distribution channels
7. "The Real Cost of Inventory" Dionco, Inc. Chicago [April 15, 2013] http://www.aadatacompany.com/actionwatch/files/The_Real_Cost_of_Inventory.pdf
8. Oechsli Institute (2011). Administrative Assistant Study. n=426 assistants and advisors from multiple distribution channels
9. Oechsli Institute and FirstClearing (2013). The Hidden Opportunities for Today's Advisor. n=721 advisors from multiple distribution channels
10. "Managing in the New World" Harvard Business Review, July–August 2009
11. Pauline W. Chen, "Can Concierge Medicine for the Few Benefit the Many?" The New York Times, August 26, 2010
12. Oechsli Institute (2008). Financial Advisor Checkup. n=847 advisors from multiple distribution channels
13. Cruise Transcript: "Get Back on Board for [Expletive] Sake!" ABC World News (January 17, 2011) http://abcnews.go.com/Blotter/transcript-italian-cruise-captain-ordered-back-boat/ story?id=15376951#.ULZ58GdT-xN
14. "Excerpts of Flight 1549 Cockpit Communications." The Associated Press [June 9, 2009] http://www.usatoday.com/news/nation/2009-06-09-hudson-cockpit-transcript_N.htm
15. Oechsli Institute and Cetera Financial (2011). Best Practices of Elite Teams. n=755 advisors from multiple distribution channels

16. Charles T. Munger, "Poor Charlie's Almanack: The Wit and Wisdom of Charles T. Munger." December 30, 2005.
17. Harriet Rubin, "C.E.O. Libraries Reveal Keys to Success." The New York Times, July 21, 2007.
18. John Coleman, "For Those Who Want to Lead, Read." HBR Blog Network, August 15, 2012. http://blogs.hbr.org/cs/2012/08/for_those_who_want_to_lead_rea.html
19. Dana Gioia, "On the Importance of Reading." http://www.csub.edu/ah/AH_matter/importanceofreading.pdf
20. Richard Perez-Pena, "Top Universities Test the Online Appeal of Free." The New York Times, July 17, 2012.
21. "Nones" on the Rise: The Pew Forum, April 15, 2013, http://www.pewforum.org/Unaffiliated/nones-on-the-rise.aspx#ranks
22. Mayo Clinic Staff, "Work-life balance: Tips to reclaim control." Mayo Clinic, July 12, 2012. http://www.mayoclinic.com/health/work-life-balance/WL00056

Index